MAD DOG COLL

First published in 1999 by Mercier Press
PO Box 5 5 French Church Street Cork
Tel: (021) 275040; Fax: (021) 274969
E-mail: books@mercier.ie
16 Hume Street Dublin 2
Tel: (01) 661 5299; Fax: (01) 661 8583
E-mail: books@marino.ie

Trade enquiries to CMD Distribution
55A Spruce Avenue
Stillorgan Industrial Park
Blackrock County Dublin
Tel: (01) 294 2556; Fax: (01) 294 2564
E.mail: cmd@columba.ie

© Breandán Delap 1999

ISBN 1 85635 291 9

10 9 8 7 6 5 4 3 2 1
A CIP record for this title is available
from the British Library

Cover design by SPACE
Printed in Ireland by ColourBooks,
Baldoyle Industrial Estate, Dublin 13

MAD DOG COLL

BREANDÁN DELAP

MERCIER PRESS

ACKNOWLEDGEMENTS

I have accumulated many debts since I started work on this book. My first and greatest is to Máire Ní Chonláin, whose boundless interest in the project from the beginning provided enthusiasm, inspiration and constant encouragement. Many thanks as well to Eimear Ní Choistealbha, Pat Comer and Celine Curtin, who provided support, criticism and companionship during my research. I am also very grateful to Sally Ní Dhuibhir, Maria Griffin-Folan and everybody at Gael Media. *Tá buíochas speisialta tuillte ag foireann Theilifís na Gaeilge a thug uchtach is spreagadh dom ón tús. Buíochas ó chroí fosta do Bhríd Rodgers agus Cáit Nic Giolla Bhríde, beirt bhan misniúil, a roinn a gcuid eolais go fial, flaithiúil liom.*

I wish to thank all at the National Archives, Northeast Region, New York, especially John Martino, whose kind assistance was invaluable. Caomhán Ó Scolaí, Antain Mac Lochlainn and John Doherty gave of their time and expertise selflessly when the book was a mere germ of an idea. I am greatly indebted to Jo O'Donoghue of Mercier Press for her advice, patience and understanding. Thanks also to Seán O'Keeffe and Linda Kenny. My parents, family and friends have been unwaveringly supportive, as have my colleagues at *Foinse*. Heartfelt thanks are due also to Robert Leibowitz, William Kennedy, T. J. English, Breandán Mac

Suibhne, Seán Mannion, Chris Campbell, Michael Bevil-
acqua, Peter Quinn, Al Pisciotta, David Rozan, Dr Mary
Farrell, Veronica Nic Giolla Bhríde, Feargal O'Gorman,
Gráinne Keegan, Seán Ó Cuirreáin, Jimmy Thadhg Mhór
Ó Baoill, Patterson Smith and Tommy DiNotte, who all
generously shared their time and knowledge with me.

Any direct quotations that appear in the book are taken
from newspapers or other contemporaneous accounts.

In no way do I wish to offend any living relatives of
Vincent Coll.

CONTENTS

INTRODUCTION

On a fresh spring night in 1962, scores of men and women from the Donegal Gaeltacht parish of Gaoth Dobhair filed into Dungloe, twelve miles away, to see a film. The quiet lisp of bicycle tyres was constant and unremitting, while courting couples stole kisses at the back of the Lough Swilly bus. Others got lifts or shared the cost of petrol. By an odd quirk of fate, the gardaí had chosen to set up a roadblock that very night and they seized the opportunity to serve summonses on those who had avoided paying car tax for decades. This particular night at the pictures was to prove costly for many.

Though the picture carried only a PG rating, the audience felt the same thrill as members of an earlier generation who had got their hands on a copy of *Lady Chatterley's Lover* or of a later one who had seen a pirated version of *The Life of Brian*. Many shifted uneasily in their seats during the screening, yet the scene is forever engraved in their memories. For the movie they went to see that night may well have been showing nationwide but it was never likely to be coming to the cinema nearest them.

On the billing in the Ritz that evening was *Mad Dog Coll,* a B-movie that barely registered a blip on the *film noir* graph. Included in its cast was an aspiring young actor named Gene Hackman, who was making his celluloid debut, alongside

Telly Savalas, in a bit part as a New York cop. Attempts to show the film some weeks previously in the Astor Cinema in Na Doirí Beaga had met with such vociferous resistance that the screening had had to be hastily cancelled.

It was in the interests of many respectable members of the Gaoth Dobhair community to ensure that the film was never shown there, just as it was in the interests of others to make the twelve-mile journey to a neighbouring parish to see it. By implying a historical continuum between the subject of the film and his living relatives, names could, and would, be blackened.

For *Mad Dog Coll* told the tale of the local boy who made bad! Entire generations of some of the most respected families in Gaoth Dobhair carried the stigma of being related to Vincent 'Mad Dog' Coll, one of the most feared gangsters in America during its 'dry' years. Others revelled in his notoriety. A figure of almost mythological status, he was referred to in hushed tones as *'an madra mire'*. Just as the Gauls refused to ever speak of their defeat by the Romans, and the names of dead pharaohs were removed from all monuments in ancient Egypt, Vincent 'Mad Dog' Coll was regarded in Gaoth Dobhair as a skeleton in the cupboard who should never be brought out. He is like a dark artery that snakes through the parish, and his life remains shrouded in secrecy. He is noticeable by his absence, for example, from all local-history publications, and most of those who could have lifted the veil on his dark secret have long since gone to their graves. In consequence his story has never been told.

Coll lived a brief and bloody life before meeting with an untimely death at the tender age of twenty-three. By that time he had acquired a fearsome reputation as public enemy number one, having had a hand in over a score of murders, including that of a five-year-old boy. He locked horns with notorious gangsters such as Dutch Schultz, Legs Diamond, Lucky Luciano, Owney Madden and Bugsy Siegel as he shot his way to a position of gangland hierarchy, leaving a stream of corpses in his wake. His gangster entourage blazed a gaudy trail across the tabloid pages of the early thirties and introduced New York to depths of depravity once thought to be the preserve of Chicago. Even the outlaws chose to outlaw him.

Coll's career defies summary. He was a murderer, bootlegger, kidnapper, hijacker, extortionist, gambler, torturer, hit man, loan shark, moonshiner, womaniser and a lot more besides. Though a shallow thinker, he had an unfettered imagination and an inflated sense of his own worth. In the absence of hard biographical evidence, most film directors have chosen to portray him as a bilious rebel without a cause or a moody malcontent suffused by evil. Yet despite his criminal reputation, he undoubtedly oozed charisma and could shock and delight with equal facility. He had a magnetic charm and could enchant a gathering with the force of his personality yet could clear a room with a mood.

Almost thirty years to the day before the film was screened in the Ritz in Dungloe, Coll had strayed into the New London Pharmacy on the south side of West Twenty-third Street, close to the plush hotel suite that he shared with his wife of five weeks. He was accompanied by a bodyguard, whose identity has never been revealed. Vincent had an important phone call to make that night. He had been blackmailing a rival gangster for some time and his patience was becoming frayed. He entered a telephone booth, dialled a number and issued a string of vile oaths into the receiver. The call was traced, however, and the recipient of his threats kept him talking for as long as possible.

Not long afterwards, three men alighted from a black limousine that had pulled up to the kerb beside the drugstore. They nodded to Coll's bodyguard, who promptly made himself absent, having already secured his thirty pieces of silver. Shards of glass filled the air like confetti as fifteen steel-jacketed slugs perforated Coll's body. Practically cleaved in half, he slumped forward as the blunt bleat of the disengaged telephone sounded a lonely requiem.

Thus ended the life of one of Gaoth Dobhair's most infamous sons. The contours of his blood-flecked career had taken him from a small fishing village in the west of Ireland to internecine mob warfare in Prohibition-era America. Dubbed 'the Mad Mick' or 'the Mad Dog', Vincent Coll cut a swathe of terror through New York society and its bootlegging underworld. Yet through the clouded prism of hindsight, people in his home parish of Gaoth Dobhair still insist that he had a good upbringing but fell into bad company over in America.

Coll was the quintessential Prohibition gangster – a European immigrant who realised that the quickest way to the American dream was via the barrel of a gun. His rise from a trough of persecution to a pedestal of power was nothing short of meteoric. Though reviled for his cruelty, newly arrived immigrants to the slums of New York must have had a sneaking regard for Coll and his accomplices, who in a few short years had amassed great wealth and influence in the teeth of sustained opposition from the white,

Anglo-Saxon establishment. On the day he was buried, the New York City Police Commissioner was even prompted to commend his hands-on approach to crime.

Nearly seventy years on, Coll continues to fascinate. In a parish that has grown used to success, he stands alone as Gaoth Dobhair's most famous historical figure. He is the subject of two B-movies (*Mad Dog Coll* and *Killer Instinct*) and full episodes of both *The Untouchables* and *The Lawless Years*. He has also cropped up from time to time in films such as *Mobsters, Billy Bathgate, The Cotton Club* and *Sleepers*. Whole Internet sites try to read apocalyptical messages into the fact that he died on Twenty-third Street at the age of twenty-three and that Dutch Schultz, the man who more than likely ordered his assasination, was himself killed on 23 October 1935, by a gunman who served twenty-three years in prison for the crime.

There are considerable conflicts in evidence, though, between official statistics and popular perceptions. Post facto legendising abounds but the facts speak eloquently for themselves. I have spoken to people who claim that Vincent returned home at the height of his glory during the Second World War, yet he had already been seven years in his grave at the outbreak of hostilities. Others remembered him at school, yet he left the country as an infant. There are many more such contradictions in the oral tradition, but the truth about Coll's life is stranger than the fiction.

1

THE HOUND OF ULSTER

Only the walls remain today of the humble homestead where the Coll seed took root. The little cottage is barely visible from the road to Bunbeg Harbour, fringed by a scrub of stunted thorn and clumps of tousled whin. It stands on a loamy hillock, commanding a fine view of Gola Island on one side and the magnificence of Errigal to the east. A rugged, craggy landscape, measled with bungalows, stretches endlessly before it. This insignificant scatter of stones, rain-pocked and furred with lichen, belies what fate had ordained for its youngest occupant.

Coll is a common surname in the three parishes that make up the Gaeltacht of north-west Donegal. Originally from Scotland, the Colls came to these shores as gallow-glasses at the beginning of the sixteenth century. After the Flight of the Earls, they settled mostly on the islands off the Donegal coast. Though times were tough, Vincent's forebears were widely regarded as very respectable, the only blot on their copybook being a reputation for land-grabbing. They had also courted unpopularity by working as bailiffs for the local landlord during the Land War. The Colls were relatively well-to-do in comparison with their neighbours.

It should be stressed, however, that Gaoth Dobhair was one of the poorest agricultural districts in the country at the time and that the family would have lived a simple existence, relying mostly on potatoes, fish and shellfish for sustenance. They were known to be both ambitious and hard-working. Locals say that the family would not sleep easily at night for fear that they would miss an opportunity for making money.

Vincent's grandfather, Tuathall Mór, earned a crust hauling goods between Bunbeg Harbour and Derry. He had come ashore from Inis Oirthear and married Bríd Ní Bhaoill from the townland of Dobhair. They made their home in the small cottage on the road to the harbour. The couple had such a large family that Tuathall was sometimes referred to as 'Tuathall na Stócach' ('Toaly of the many children'). Some time towards the end of the nineteenth century, he bought a pub in Machaire Clochair from a neighbour who was keen to offload it to purchase his fare to Australia. This establishment, now known as Tigh Hiúdaí Beag, is one of the most renowned watering holes in Ireland, having spawned such musical talent as Clannad and Altan. Tuathall bequethed it to his son Donie Thuathall, a future magistrate who would cross swords in 1905 with a young lawyer named Patrick Pearse when he presided over the celebrated prosecution of Niall Mac Giolla Bhríde, whose only crime was to have his name and address written in Irish on his cart. Old people in the area still refer to the pub as 'Tigh Dhonie'.

Vincent's father, Tuathall Óg, or Toaly, was born in 1868 and eked out a modest existence as a farmer before emigrating to America in 1892, where he took up residence at 686 Myrtle Avenue, Brooklyn. There he met Anna Mary Duncan, who was six years his junior. She had been born in

Dublin in 1874 to an Irish father, Thomas Duncan, and an Australian mother, Mary Reilly. Toaly and Anna were married, after a short period of courtship, and a girl, Florence, was born to them in 4 November 1893.

It was at this stage that the Coll family decided to return to Toaly's home in Gaoth Dobhair, which he had recently inherited. It seems extraordinary that Toaly should return to Gaoth Dobhair after such a short stay in America, particularly when his new bride was not even from the area. In those days there would have been an American wake for those who emigrated, in the knowledge that they were very unlikely ever to set foot in the country again. Most of Toaly's siblings had also emigrated to America and Australia, and none of them ever returned. There is no explanation as to why the young couple would have chosen to return. Neither is there any evidence to suggest that they had amassed enough wealth during their few short years abroad to live happily ever after in the country of their birth.

On their return from exile, Toaly and Anna took up residence in the modest family homestead on the road to Bunbeg Harbour. Sadly, their first son, Toal, died in 1896 at the age of two of scarlet fever. The harsh, damp conditions of the western seaboard made no exceptions for the young Coll family, and another boy, Robert, met with the same fate as the new century unspooled. Four boys did survive, however – Thomas (born 1898), Charles (1903), Peter (1907) and Vincent, who was born on 20 July 1908. With the exception of Thomas, who is registered as having been born in the family home in Bunbeg, all the other Coll boys were officialy born in Machaire Clochair, the neighbouring townland. Some locals have it that Vincent was born in Tigh

Hiúdaí Beag, his uncle Donie's pub, in Machaire Clochair. Its more sanitary conditions were presumably thought to make the pub more suitable for the rigours of childbirth than the family's own small, overcrowded cottage. There is no evidence to substantiate this claim, however, and Coll's relatives insist that he was born in the family home near Bunbeg Harbour. Besides, the village of Bunbeg was often interchangeable with the electoral district of Machaire Clochair in official documents.

The eldest children, Florence, Thomas and Charles, attended the local primary school at Cnoc a' Stollaire, just over a mile away from their house. Though English was the language of tuition at the time, Irish was the language of the schoolyard. It is reasonable to assume, therefore, that the eldest children would have been fluent Irish speakers, although Irish may not have been spoken at home, as their mother, Anna, was not a native speaker and may not have been very proficient in the language. It is likely, though, that Vincent himself might have had a *cúpla focal,* particularly in light of the fact that he later ended up under the guardianship of another Gaoth Dobhair woman, his aunt Mary Friel.

Historian Breandán Mac Suibhne contends that the Gaoth Dobhair Vincent Coll was born into was an essentially violent society. The previous two generations had seen periods of serious social unrest, and Mac Suibhne believes that there was a glamourisation of violence in the area as a result. Attempts by the local landlord, Lord George Hill, to introduce black-faced sheep and Scottish shepherds to the parish between 1857 and 1860 precipitated such widespread anarchy that 300 policemen had to be drafted into the area to keep order. Thirty years later, Gaoth Dobhair was again thrown into chaos when District Inspector William Martin was bludgeoned to death by an angry mob as he tried to arrest the parish priest, Canon James McFadden, to answer a charge of incitement. It must be emphasised, however, that these incidents, though bloody and barbaric, were the culmination of years of land agitation – unlike the savage acts of casual violence that characterised Vincent Coll's rise to notoriety in the 1930s.

Six months after Vincent first saw the light of day, the family decided to up and leave once again and return to America. Toaly had tried, without success, to work the yieldless ground and eventually threw his hat at it in exasperation. There is some suggestion too that he may have accumulated large gambling debts and squandered whatever modest wealth the family had. The Colls had been cheating time, moving back and forth from nineteenth- and twentieth-century America to a country several light years behind. Though seasonal migration between Gaoth Dobhair and Scotland was very common at the time, the Coll family's return to America was highly irregular and contrary to all conventional patterns. Once again, it is unclear why they decided to go back to New York. If they had not succeeded in making a fist of it before, was there any real chance of increased success the second time around? Could it have been that Anna had found it difficult to settle in Gaoth Dobhair, or had the death of their two sons prompted the couple to seek better conditions abroad? We can only speculate.

On 3 April 1909, Toaly and Anna took their young clutch to Derry and boarded the steamship SS *Columbia*, bound for New York.

2

MAD DOGS AND IRISHMEN

The *Columbia* docked in New York on 12 April 1909 after a
nine-day crossing. The Coll family, having already spent
some time in the US, were discharged on the pier and spared
the rigours of an Ellis Island inquisition. They settled initially
at 55 East Twenty-second Street, the Bronx, before setting
up home in a cold-water tenement at 555 Westchester
Avenue, in the same borough.

By the time the Colls arrived on the scene the ethnic
make-up of the Bronx was predominantly German and Irish.
The rural Irish were still a peasant caste in New York in the
early years of this century; their horizons severely restricted
by the white, Anglo-Saxon, Protestant establishment. They
had come from the most primitive agricultural situation in
Europe to the most rapidly industialising society in the world
and had been slow to adjust to the demands of their new
environment. Contrary to popular perception, it took the
Irish longer than almost any other ethnic group to assimilate
into mainstream American society. Writing in the 1890s,
the great reformer Jacob Riïs categorised the Irish as the
permanent inhabitants of tenements, an underclass who had
internalised their poverty and were unable to pull themselves

up on the American ladder of success. Though the colour of their skin was no barrier to assimilation, Irish immigrants fought their own battles for acceptance. They were distrusted by the Protestant ruling classes, who perceived their allegiance to a foreign Pope as treacherous and disloyal. Thus as Peter Quinn notes in *How the Irish Stayed Irish*, 'Religion – not colour – became the line of demarcation.'

Modern 'mobocracy' in America can be said to have had its genesis in the tolerant disregard the unassimilated European immigrants had for the forces of law and order in what they perceived as a rigidly stratified society. This was particularly the case in the migrant melting pot of the Bronx. The borough's heady mix of sprawling slums and flyblown gin mills was to prove to be the ideal breeding ground for anyone who was not prepared to let morality stand in the way of social mobility. In the words of author Graham Nown, the only sure way to the American Dream was to 'get a break in the movies, the Mets or the Mob'. Flourishing under police protection, notorious gangs ruled the streets of the Bronx, marauding with abandon amongst the clapboard houses, grog shops, slaughterhouses, railroad yards and gasworks. The area was distinguishable by its dull, mon-otonous ugliness; droves of filth-encrusted kids thronged the steamy, fetid streets, hawking petty goods, pickpocketing, keeping pigeons on tenement roofs and taking an occasional dip in the Hutchinson and Bronx Rivers. Such was the rugged environment that spawned Vincent Coll.

In many ways, the fate of the Coll family can be seen as a microcosm of the hardship endured by new arrivals to the US in general. The Colls were the flip side of the American Dream, unable to eke out an existence at home and finding the land of hope and opportunity to be something of a closed shop. The empty husks of their dreams are to be seen in Kensico and St Raymond's Cemeteries. None of the Coll boys lived to the age of twenty-five; ailments of the lung, brought on by horrendous living conditions, accounted for two of them. Of the whole brood, only Florence lived to see middle age.

On 12 February 1916 Anna Coll, Vincent's long-suffering mother, passed away. She had lived a sad and torturous life. Allied to the harrowing experience of losing two of her children in Donegal, a baby girl, who had been born to the couple shortly after their arrival in the US, died of dysentery aged just nine months. Anna appears to have received very little support in her efforts to provide for her children amid numbing poverty and declining health.

A report by the Bronx Catholic Big Brothers League described her as being 'industrious and in every respect a good mother' but stressed that she was so overworked and undernourished that she suffered from some sort of scrofulous disease. This illness resulted in running sores on various parts of her body; the sores appeared from time to time but left no scars. She eventually died of lobar pneumonia and 'general weakness' at the age of forty-two. She was buried in Kensico Cemetery, in a plot that her brother, Peter Duncan, had purchased for $400 at the turn of the century. This was no mean sum at the time and suggests that Duncan was fairly well-off. It would appear, however, that he did not see fit to offer his sister any financial assistance that might have alleviated her hardship.

The death of his mother was presumably a shattering blow for young Vincent, who was only seven years old at the time. But worse was to follow. On 15 December 1920 his brother Charles died of tuberculosis after a protracted illness. Charles was seventeen years old and had been working as a waiter in Staten Island. Two months later, Vincent's eldest brother, Thomas, who had worked as an attendant at the Middleton State Homeopathic Hospital in Orange County, died, also of tuberculosis, at the tender age of twenty-three. In a society where peer survival was at a premium, five of Vincent's siblings had died before he had reached the age of twelve. In such a world, it may well have been that Vincent himself did not expect to see old age and had therefore set out, subconsciously at least, to achieve everything he could in his youth.

With tongue wedged firmly in cheek, Vincent Coll's second cousin, Assemblywoman Bríd Rodgers of the SDLP, tells how she was always led to believe as a child that Mad Dog's bad blood had come from the maternal side of his family. The truth, sadly, was probably somewhat different. Though the scant historical documents available raise more questions than they answer, it can be inferred from contemporary death certificates and census forms that Toaly Coll was not exactly an ideal father. Like many other Irish immigrants at the time, he was essentially a peasant farmer and lacked the labour skills demanded by America's industry-driven society.

A report by the Bronx Catholic Big Brothers League refers to him as a lazy drunkard who 'never made any real effort to support his family'. Though the league speculated that Toaly died of diabetes and tuberculosis at the age of forty-nine, there is no record of his death in the New York State Board of Heath Index, nor does he share a grave with his wife or offspring. What happened to Toaly is a matter of conjecture. Old people in Gaoth Dobhair have told me that he remarried a woman from the townland of Mín an Iolair called Biddy Thomáis Bhilly, who spent her last years back in the parish after Toaly had passed away. There is no evidence, documentary or otherwise, to subtantiate this claim, however.

What we can be sure of is that Toaly fled the nest, leaving his phalanx of young sons as good as orphaned in the teeming squalor of the Bronx. Students of psychoanalysis may point to the protracted absence of a father figure as a seminal factor in the configuration of events that led to a young Gaoth Dobhair man becoming one of the most-feared mobsters ever to roam the streets of New York. Could his violence be seen as a sign of some deeply repressed childhood trauma or unresolved inner conflict? Was he permanently scarred by the conflicts of his formative years? It should be pointed out, however, that Vincent Coll was not the only poor immigrant boy to have come from a broken home and that he displayed extreme psychopathic symptoms that stretched the boundaries of a dysfunctional childhood. There were many poor Irish immigrants, but there was only one Mad Dog Coll.

Vincent's psychological and physical reports make disturbing reading. A cogent pattern emerges of a young boy, uprooted and rudderless, struggling to cope with the rigours of a hostile and alien environment. His first years in America had been characterised by great deprivation, unrelieved poverty, parental discord, social dislocation, illness and neglect. He appears to have been a delicate child and was chronically constipated during his teenage years. He had dull hearing and though he had twenty-twenty vision his eyes did not align properly. He often went unfed and unclothed and grew up largely unprotected in the exacting environment of the streets.

The forces that moulded his errant behaviour cannot easily be determined. Though he was undoubtedly a victim of circumstance, the theory that a life of crime was forced upon him by his repressed, impoverished background does not account fully for the lust for blood and torture that he displayed during his adult years. In gangster parlance, he had a bloody mouth, appearing to revel in murder as a form of entertainment. Unlike other gang leaders, Coll had a hands-on approach to crime and liked to do the job himself; it was as though committing a crime filled him with a sense of power or joy.

Many in Gaoth Dobhair suggest that Vincent had a good upbringing but fell into bad company in New York. They believe he was a victim of circumstance and went bad through his association with other criminals. 'Rinne an saol i Meiriceá crosta á,' Cáit Nic Giolla Bhríde told me. ('Life in America made him troublesome.') Equally, another relative, Jimmy Thadhg Mhór Ó Baoill, believed that Coll was led astray by the company he kept. 'Thit sé isteach i ndroch-chuideachta inteacht thall i Meiriceá. Ní shílím go bhfuair sé drochthógáil óna mhuintir,' he told me. ('He fell into bad company in America. I don't think he had a bad upbringing.') Although others in Gaoth Dobhair would echo these sentiments, there is little evidence that Vincent Coll was easily cowed or led.

Coll's violent nature would probably suggest that he had a sociopathic and psychopathic personality, but the fact that he suffered from petit mal epilepsy and bouts of dizziness as a child raise the possibility that his problems may have been organic. The symptoms of petit mal epilepsy are absences or momentary lapses in awareness and are so brief and subtle that the condition may go unrecognized or be mistakenly attributed to daydreaming. Vincent's epilepsy may have been hereditary or he may have developed it due to lack of oxygen or other complications during his birth.

More telling, perhaps, are the results of a psychogram carried out on behalf of the New York State Reformatory in 1927. This test concluded that Coll was a 'constitutional psychopathic inferior' who was 'unfit for his liberty'. It also suggested that he showed 'some resemblance to dementia praecox' – now known as schizophrenia – and that he might 'develop insanity at any time'. Coll certainly displayed all the characteristics of a schizophrenic. There was undoubtedly a progressive deterioration in his personality and he exhibited disorders of feeling, thought and conduct.

The actions that led to his noteriety would suggest that he had difficulty coping with problems relating to human relationships and that he was incapable of responding to influence and suggestion. He was also of course a master of mood swings and showed little empathy with others. Allied to this, Vincent displayed shallow and inappropriate emotional responses and harboured false perceptions and delusions. These are all classic symptoms of schizophrenia. The validity of the New York State Reformatory report is questionable, however, and it is impossible to carry out a psychological autopsy on Coll seventy years after his death. What we can be certain of, though, is that he would have received very little, if any, treatment for his illnesses in the various institutions that, from the age of seven, he bounced in and out of.

After their mother's death Vincent and his brother Peter

were privately placed in the Mission of the Immaculate Virgin (Mount Loretto) on Staten Island by their uncle Peter Duncan. The mission was set up in the 1880s by the Catholic Church as a shelter for homeless and disabled children. The institution still stands to this day, flanked by a magnificent mosaic of meadows, wetlands and woods and an impressive waterfront. Its boarded-up granite façade has an eerie air about it, befitting a place that has seen much sadness.

The three decades after the famine had seen a massive influx of Irish into New York, and the number of destitute immigrant children in the city had reached alarming proportions. The authorities believed that these 'armies of the street' could be cured of their deviancy if they were shipped off to the Western states and fostered out to good, upstanding Protestants. The Church therefore saw the establishment of institutions like the Mission of the Immaculate Virgin as a necessary way of regulating their own delinquents – a Catholic solution to a Catholic problem, so to speak. The mission was run with a heavy hand of discipline and aimed to break the kids' street habits. What it actually achieved, however, was to breed successive generations of professional toughs.

Vincent remained in the mission for three unhappy years, running away on several occasions before being taken to live with his aunt Mary Friel at 357 East 150th Street, the Bronx, in the area now known as the Hub. Conditions in the cold-water railroad flat that Vincent and Peter shared with their aunt would have been Spartan. The boys' cousin Anna Freiss and her husband, Walter, lived there as well, along with their son, who died in infancy of 'marasmus due to artificial feeding'.

Vincent's relationship with his aunt appears to have been strained at the best of times, and she had great difficulty keeping him on the straight and narrow. He was clearly a very troubled and troublesome child. Such was the extent of his unruliness that Mary Friel deemed it necessary to bring him to the Bronx Children's Court on 16 August 1920 for stealing money from her and repeatedly running away from home. She claimed that he was 'an ungovernable child'. Once again Vincent was committed to the Mission of the Immaculate Virgin, but he broke out shortly after his arrival and was deemed 'incorrigible' by the director.

As relations between Vincent and his aunt soured, it fell upon Coll's older sister, Florence, to act as a surrogate mother to him. Florence was fifteen years his senior and made all the important decisions for the family. She was cold and emotionally detached and did not share her little brother's good looks. In fact, she had all the appearances of a vinegar-faced spinster and had huge bags under her eyes. Contemporaneous newspaper accounts refer to her as 'Amazonian'. She had an acid tongue and her speech was frequently larded with expletives. Rather than setting a good example for her wayward brothers, Florence and her husband, Joe Reddan, were as deeply embroiled in crime as Vincent and Peter.

If survival of the fittest was the name of the game in the ermine-lined hell-hole of the Bronx, then young Vincent Coll was more than up to the challenge. By the time he reached his teenage years he had a brace of felonies under his belt and a substantial criminal reputation. He was a tall, mop-headed boy with a fuss of soft curls and was both taut-muscled and rangy. He showed an utter contempt for the social order or authority and there was little he would not do in pursuit of a quick buck. He displayed leadership qualities from an early age and exuded a briny confidence at all times. It is a mark of Coll's status that he had risen to the rank of gang leader by his early twenties. Other members of his gang were more than ten years his senior but nonetheless bowed to Coll's authority. Though a year older than Vincent, his brother Peter perpetually dwelt in his shadow and was never more than a dot below Vincent's great exclamation mark.

While under the guardianship of his aunt, Vincent attended Public School Number 9, near Brook Avenue, the Bronx, in 1923. He was enrolled in sixth grade for a total of fifty-three days but missed nineteen of these through a combination of illness and truancy. He did not distinguish himself there and his schoolwork was described as 'not very satisfactory and barely passable'. He returned to the school for a few days in 1924 to receive his employment certificate, which was given to him with some reluctance. It would appear that Vincent may have later progressed as far as eighth grade while incarcerated at Randall's Island. It is impossible to ascertain what level of education he attained but we can reasonably assume that his years of detention had equipped him with at least a rudimentary grasp of the three 'R's. This, however, was probably the apogee of his scholastic achievement.

None of the future members of Coll's gang were exactly Mensa material, and at least one of them, the diminutive Tuffy Odierno, was completely illiterate. Coll may indeed have been the man with one eye in the kingdom of the blind, for although many of his exploits were audacious and daring, he was by and large impulsive, reckless and indiscreet. All told, he was an intellectual nullity who relied on heavy-handed tactics to enforce his reign of terror and showed contemptuous disregard for anyone who happened to get in his way.

If there are few records of Coll's scholastic achievements, accounts of his extramural activities are numerous. By his early teens, he had become the scourge of the east Bronx, wreaking havoc and exacting tributes from street vendors. His notoriety grew rapidly. He displayed a strutting confidence, believing that anything that took his fancy was his for the taking. With the aid of Peter, he set up extortion rackets, smashing windows and stealing goods from those who declined to avail of his services. He acted without thinking, purely on reflex, issuing blood-curdling threats to anyone who questioned his authority.

Coll also built up a reputation as a vicious combatant, using a vast array of dangerous weapons to silence his enemies. These weapons included broken bottles, switch-blades, brass knuckles, rocks, clubs, guns and stockings packed with sand or flour. A sketch in the movie *Mobsters* depicts a typical street scene in tenement New York at the beginning of the century: a young hood muscles in on a lucrative game of crap, seizing the pot and taking to his heels, several dollars richer. This ploy was to become particularly associated with the Gaoth Dobhair man, whose gangling gait made for an effortless getaway.

A report by the Bronx Catholic Big Brothers League in 1926 noted that Vincent 'spared no pains to gain the applause of the worst element among boys of the neighbourhood.' Amongst his teenage cronies were Mike and Fiore Basile, Dominic Odierno, Louis Bifano and Pasquele del Greco –

all future members of his gang. But the young Coll was not always inclusive in his play. He took a particular aversion to an older Jewish boy whom he regarded as 'a slob and a yellow rat'. The boy, whose name was Arthur Flegenheimer, was later known as Dutch Schultz and would be instrumental in Coll's rise to power and ultimately in his death.

By his early teens, Coll exhibited extremely violent tendencies and had a string of felonies to his name. He rapidly developed into a hard-bitten thug with complete contempt for authority. On 16 September 1920 he appeared in the Children's Court charged with 'forcibly entering a booth and stealing'. Having being rejected by the mission, he was committed to the New York Catholic Protectory – an infamously rough residential institution that had been untouched by the liberal reform movement. There Vincent joined up with his older brother, Peter, and the two youngsters looked out for one another and formed an inseparable bond. Predictably enough, Vincent broke out of the protectory three times. On the last such occasion, Florence, aware of his imminent parole, returned him to the institution.

By the time he was fifteen, Vincent was on an endless treadmill of crime and violence and had virtually earned a season ticket to the Children's Court. He ran away from home twice – an indication, if any were needed, that his relationship with his guardian was less than harmonious. Some time in 1923 he contracted tuberculosis and was sent to the Municipal Sanatorium at Otisville to recuperate. He must have feared the worst, as two of his brothers had already died of a similar ailment a few years previously. But not even ill-health could contain the wayward spirit of Vincent

Coll. He ran away from the sanatorium and slept rough for a number of weeks. Miraculously, he survived the harsh conditions of winter, and on 13 December 1923 he was arraigned again as 'an ungovernable child' and remanded to the Metropolitan Hospital. He had recovered sufficiently by February 1924 to be released under the supervision of his sister, Florence, at her house at 1759 Montgomery Avenue, the Bronx.

But Vincent was soon in trouble again. He was fortunate to escape being sent down for another term when he and a teenage accomplice were caught robbing a store of two packs of Camels. He pushed his luck, though, when he stole a Ford coupe worth $450, a sum that made the crime a grand larceny. As he was still under the age of fifteen, he avoided being tried on a felony charge by the criminal courts and appeared instead before the Children's Court, a familiar hunting ground, on 12 May 1924. Deceived by his angelic countenance, the presiding judge turned a blind eye to Coll's high rate of recidivism and placed him on probation instead of returning him to the reformatory. Though Coll was still in poor health, Florence found it difficult to keep him indoors and complained to her brother's probation officer that he was keeping late hours. The subsequent reprimand fell on deaf ears, as Vincent took to his heels once more in September 1924.

Coll's luck soon ran out, though, and on 20 November 1924 Judge Daniel F. Murphy sent him to the House of Refuge at Randall's Island for an indeterminate term on his guilty plea to a violation of Section 1897 of the Penal Laws (possession of a revolver). But inmate #35973 once again proved hard to contain. On Independence Day 1926 he escaped from the institution but was recaptured five hours later when he returned to his old neighbourhood. His conduct record at the house of refuge was appalling, covering practically every infraction of the rules. Such was the scale of his unruliness that on 5 August 1926 the Board of Managers of the Society for the Reformation of Juvenile Delinquents in the City of New York deemed it necessary to file a petition to the Supreme Court applying for his transfer to a more suitable correctional institution. In his affidavit to the court, Louis Crolly, Acting Superintendent of the House of Refuge, stated that Coll was 'not amenable to the discipline' imposed at the institution and that he openly resisted 'the lawful authority of the officers'. Furthermore, Crolly declared that Coll repeatedly exerted 'a dangerous and pernicious influence over the other inmates' and that he did not appear 'to have benefited from the reformative influence of the House of Refuge'.

As he had reached his eighteenth birthday a couple of weeks earlier, the Supreme Court decided on 9 August 1926 that Coll should be transferred to the New York State Reformatory at Elmira in upstate New York. Elmira prided itself on being an institution that was more rehabilitative than punitive. When it opened its doors in 1876, the prison was hailed as a humane solution to crime and a panacea for the assorted ills of American society. In this regard it should be regarded as an abject failure.

In his in-depth study of the American penal system, Alexander W. Pisciotta suggests that, while Elmira promised benevolent reform, it delivered benevolent repression. Inmates were whipped with rubber hoses and two-foot leather straps and restricted to bread and water in dark dungeons during months of solitary confinement. The reformatory was hopelessly overcrowded, and a report by the New York State Board of Charities concluded that 'evil' homosexual activity was rampant, declaring that 'The licentiousness shown to have existed in the reformatory at Elmira, and for which the system of "doubling up" is largely responsible, is so vile as to be almost incredible of belief.'

An elaborate military drilling system involving wooden rifles was introduced, and infibulation – the insertion of a ring in the foreskin of the penis – was practised in an attempt to curb masturbation. The institution attempted to pummel its inmates into submission and believed that it could transform them into fine, upstanding American citizens by instilling in them the Protestant work ethic. The bulk of offenders were of European extraction, however, and were mainly Catholic or Jewish. These inmates reacted badly to Elmira's draconian regime, which was designed to assimilate them fully into mainstream American society rather than accommodate their ethnicity.

The harshness of the institution's regime can be gauged by an incident that occurred in April 1930, when the lawyer Samuel S. Leibowitz, who later successfully defended Coll, informed the Kings County Court that one of his clients would rather be sent to the infamous Sing Sing prison for a number of years than to Elmira for a few months. We must assume that Coll, as one of the worst-behaved prisoners ever to enter the institution's portals, was subjected to a wide range of abuse in Elmira.

In the early years of this century a clear distinction emerged in Elmira between salvageable offenders, who participated in a variety of rehabilitative programmes, and 'mentally defective' offenders, who underwent an incapacitative-custodial regime aimed at protecting the public at large. Vincent Coll was placed firmly in the latter category by virtue of a report that the Bronx Catholic Big Brothers League had submitted at the time of his admission to Elmira. The league had supervised Vincent after his release from the New York Catholic Protectory and concluded that Coll was a 'mental defective', that is to say that he was biologically and psychologically inferior and not amenable to reform. He was, in other words, regarded as being beyond redemption. Small wonder then, in light of such reckless stigmatising, that instead of undergoing a Damascene conversion, Coll honed his criminal skills and knowledge during his years in detention.

The authorities in Elmira concluded that Vincent had poor learning ability, was ill-informed and had 'little interest in anything outside of his gangster activities'. In a classic understatement, they also surmised that he had 'poor ethical sense'. Allied to this, he was described as 'a dependent type' who was 'lazy and shiftless' and had poor industrial capacity. The report suggested that a spell in the army might do him the power of good – unless he was 'disqualified by temperament' – but concluded that he should be 'watched carefully'. With such a glowing reference, Vincent was paroled in 1927.

If, as Dostoevsky asserts, 'the standards of a nation's civilisation can be judged by opening the doors of its prisons', then American society, through its repressive penal system, failed Vincent Coll. Although Coll's alienation had forced him out of society, it did not logically follow that his further alienation through the penal system would force him back into it. In many ways he was a product of a social structure that was incapable of dealing with children who had behavioural problems. Vincent was certainly not a hardened criminal when he began his institutional life at the age of seven, but by the time he left he certainly was. Most of his formative years were spent in some institution or other and it is true to say that during this time he developed violent antisocial behaviour and a serious disrespect for authority – as well as falling in with his future cronies, of course.

After his parole, Vincent soon retired to the netherworld of brainless skulduggery from which he had briefly surfaced. On 13 December 1928 he was arrested under the name of Vincent Donohue for unlawful entry in the Bronx, but he was subsequently discharged by the presiding magistrate. Two weeks later, on St Stephen's Day, he was arrested once more in the Bronx for assault and robbery but was discharged again. Undeterred, and perhaps buoyed up by his successful scrapes with the law, Coll soon fell foul of the authorities once more. He was arrested in Yonkers as a suspicious person and sent back to Elmira to finish his term.

By the time Coll saw the light of day again, in 1929, he had grown into a handsome, rangy young man with fine flaxen locks, blond-lashed blue eyes and delicate cheekbones. A dusting of freckles across a prowlike nose and a toothsome grin completed his choirboy image.

But history had contrived to overtake Coll during his period of detention. Prohibition, the greatest social experiment in American history, had been ushered in, and many people were becoming rich on the back of it, no one more so than Coll's childhood adversary – Dutch Schultz.

3

A Dog's Body

On the stroke of midnight on 16 January 1920, the United States of America dried up – and also, paradoxically, went on the biggest binge in the history of mankind. By prohibiting the manufacture, sale or transportation of intoxicating liquors, the Eighteenth Amendment to the Constitution took the drinks trade out of the hands of honest businessmen and presented the criminal fraternity with a conduit to prosperity. As an experiment in regulating the social behaviour of its populace, it was an abject failure, as hitherto-compliant citizens flagrantly flouted the law of the land.

The Volstead Act contained many holes, through which alcohol continued to pour. Drink could still be stored in bonded warehouses and could be prescribed by doctors for medicinal purposes. Moreover, smugglers had 18,700 miles of largely unpatrolled American border to slip across. A contemporary commentator noted that Prohibition went into effect at midnight on 16 January 1920 and that the first illegal drink was served about a minute later. Thus the *New York Times*'s bleak headline 'John Barleycorn Died Peacefully at the Toll of 12' proved unfounded.

The fact of the matter was that Americans drank alcohol

in far greater quantities during Prohibition than in any other period of the country's history. This prompted the humorist Will Rogers to remark that 'Prohibition is better than no liquor at all.'

Prohibition combined the evangelical spirit of the Pilgrim Fathers with the witch-hunting fanaticism of the Salem elders. For nearly half a century, the Women's Christian Temperance Movement, along with religious leaders of the day, had been fighting the evils of liquor. Edward Behr, author of *Prohibition: Thirteen Years that Changed America*, traces the origin of Prohibition to the teachings of the temperance movement in colonial times. In these zealous circles, intoxication was regarded as a worse affliction than tuberculosis, as it infected the mind as well as the body. Behr suggests that Prohibition was the rearguard action of the New England WASPs, who were concerned about the massive influx of immigrants from poor European countries, where drink was a part of the culture. They believed that they were witnessing the disintegration of the fabric of society as they knew it. In that sense, Prohibition was a last-ditch effort by the self-appointed guardians of traditional values to save village America from the inevitable march of time. Far from driving the European immigrant communities into Anglo-Saxon conformity, however, Prohibition consolidated these groups' position. The bootlegging business in New York, for example, was half Jewish, a quarter Italian, an eighth Polish and an eighth Irish. The Anglo-Saxon elite were reduced to the role of consumers, while the recent emigrants became entrepreneurs.

A fine line developed between law-abiding and law-breaking, as those engaged in the illicit liquor trade were seen to be servicing a demand. 'When I sell liquor it's bootlegging. When my patrons serve it on a silver tray on Lake Shore Drive, it's hospitality,' Al Capone famously declared. Dutch Schultz was equally forthcoming in his rejection of the tag of public enemy number one: 'I never did anything to deserve that, unless it was to supply good beer to people who wanted it.' Other bootleggers, like Jack 'Legs' Diamond, achieved celebrity status on the strength of their illegal trading practices and were fêted lavishly on their trips abroad.

Large breweries like Anheuser-Busch decided to concentrate their expertise in the production of 'near-beer', which was below the legal limit of 0.5 per cent alcohol. As Will Rogers, the wag for all occasions, commented, 'After drinking a bottle of this near-beer, you have to take a glass of water as a stimulant.' Anything less than the real McCoy was clearly not an option!

Inevitably the most striking by-product of Prohibition was the diminution of respect for the institutions of law and order and for those who administered it. Mobsters became rich fast, while corruption in the police force was endemic. When the dust settled and the amendment was finally repealed, in 1933, America was left with a social hangover that has dogged it to this day. Prohibition was essentially the take-off point for organised crime in America; the seeds of most of the identifiable crime empires of today took root during this era. Running large-scale convoys of booze required extraordinary powers of organisation as the trickle of smuggled alcohol developed into a tidal wave and bootlegging grew from a cottage industry into a corporate enterprise. When the curtain eventually came down on

Prohibition, the crime barons channelled their expertise and considerable wealth into gambling, prostitution and drug-smuggling empires.

*

One of the most successful men to have ridden the prosperity curve of Prohibition was Arthur Flegenheimer, alias Dutch Schultz – Coll's childhood foe. Of all the gangsters of the period, the Dutchman has received the harshest portrayal on celluloid. He is depicted as an obnoxious megalomaniac who was prone to mood swings and verged on the psychopathic. He gave bad taste a bad name. A small, globular man, he had a puffy face, shadowy eyes and a flinty stare. Every anti-Semitic stereotype has been heaped upon him over the years, and contemporary accounts do little to dispel them. He was a chillingly self-absorbed man, reviled in the underworld, who brutally disposed of anyone who challenged his authority. He appears to have had few redeeming qualities.

Schultz was born into a Lower East Side ghetto at 1690 Second Avenue, off Eighty-ninth Street, on 6 August 1902. Like Coll, he had a dysfunctional relationship with his father, Herman, who took to his heels in 1910, leaving his wife and young clutch to fend for themselves. In his formative years, Arthur received a grounding in delinquency from the Bergen Gang of pickpockets and store thieves, whom he joined at an early age. His mother, Emma Neu Fleggenheimer, doted and lavished affection on him and bought a pushcart to sell pickles in order to subsidise his wardrobe. Like Coll's aunt, Mary Friel, she was unable to control the movements of her wayward son, but that she brooked no suggestions of impropriety on his part. She moved her family to the Lower Bronx, where Arthur attended Public School 12. There he showed some scholarly promise, particularly in history and composition. His mother was at the end of her tether trying to curb his truancy, though, and even went so far as to ask the school principal, Dr John F. 'Jafsie' Condon, to intervene by visiting their home. In spite of the encouragement the boy received, sixth grade seems to have been the apogee of Schultz's scholastic attainment.

By an odd quirk of chance, Condon later rose to prominence as an intermediary in the Lindbergh baby kidnapping of 1932, when he famously tossed the $50,000 ransom money over the wall in St Raymond's Cemetery, the Bronx, where Vincent Coll had been interred a week previously. It seems that St Raymond's Cemetery was a happening place in the spring of 1932!

In a rare moment of expansiveness, during his tax trial in Syracuse in the spring of 1935, Schultz informed an attentive posse of journalists that he had had to quit school at the age of fourteen to help support his family. 'It was tough bucks them days,' he declared. He worked briefly as a paper boy and a printer's devil and was plying his trade in composition roofing at the time of his first arrest for burglary, at the age of seventeen. He was to be arrested on twelve other occasions before eventually being killed in a Newark steakhouse in October 1935. He was convicted in December 1919 of cleaning out an apartment in the Grand Concourse and sent to Blackwell's Island Penitentiary for an indeterminate term. He was later transferred to Westhampton Prison Farms, near Goshen, from which he soon escaped. He was recaptured within fifteen hours and served fifteen months in total – the only time he was to spend in a correctional institution. Rather than his spell in jail bringing his errant nature to heel, Schultz emerged from custody a bitter, twisted man with a finely tuned aptitude for the nefarious.

The proceeds of a number of previous robberies enabled Arthur to finance the purchase of an enormous saloon in the Bronx. It was around this time that he decided that a change of name was in order. In his compelling study of Jewish gangsters, *Tough Jews,* Rich Cohen theorises that every kid who makes his way in the New York underworld inherits a tradition of gang warfare that spans several centuries, 'as even the lowliest bush-league baseball player inherits the mantle of Gehrig and Ruth'. Cohen draws links between the Prohibition-era gangsters and their counterparts of the previous century and concludes that, for living gangsters, the stories of dead gangsters and the weight of their legacy is the only history that amounts to much. Thus when Arthur Flegenheimer assumed the sobriquet of Dutch Schultz, after an infamous pugilist from the nineteenth-century Frog Hollow gang, he had completed his underworld bar mitzvah. Besides, as he himself used to boast, Arthur Flegenheimer was too long a name to appear in the headlines of the metropolitan dailies.

In 1928 Schultz formed a business partnership with Joey Noe and set up the Hub Social Club, an extremely profitable speakeasy in a Brook Avenue tenement. The partners' ill-gotten gains helped finance several other illicit outlets, which they supplied with hijacked or smuggled liquor from Canada or Europe and with Schultz's own home-brewed potion. Within a year, Schultz & Noe owned a chain of speakeasies, a fleet of trucks and several beer-drops for storing the booze. To protect their assets and persuade others of their merit as suppliers, Schultz and Noe set about recruiting some of the toughest henchmen ever to roam the streets of New York. Although Vincent Coll had not as yet entered the fold, Schultz's ranks included some of the city's most notorious crime figures, including Bo Weinberg and Joey Rao, both of whom were to play a significant role in Coll's fall from grace and possibly in his death. Schultz's formidable band of thugs set about eliminating the opposition as their operation fanned out across Manhattan and the Bronx.

The Dutchman also formed an association of restaurateurs. Those who joined were guaranteed no trouble but had to pay as much as $25,000 for the privilege. Anyone who failed to pay the tribute could expect to have their premises stink-bombed.

Towards the end of 1920s, Schultz had his eye on another bounty. The numbers racket or policy – a primitive form of the lottery – had heretofore been the preserve of the black mobsters of Harlem. In the impoverished era of the Great Depression, for many people a winning-numbers slip was the only chance to put food on the table. Each day thousands of people picked a three-digit number. The winning number paid back at odds of 600 to 1. Thus a cent could earn $6 and a dime $60. It was a multimillion-dollar business, and Schultz sniffed an opening. He presented Stephanie St Clair, the undisputed queen of the numbers in Harlem, with his own variety of Hobson's choice: hand over her operation or face the cataclysmic alternative. St Clair succumbed and the other Harlem policy kings capitulated like a house of cards.

Schultz was soon a millionare several times over, though

his friends and relations were not exactly made flush by his munificence. As well as being a major player in the slot-machine business, he was the 'Beer Baron of the Bronx' and king of Harlem's numbers racket and had established a monopoly over much of the New York liquor trade. Loathsome and repellent he may have been, but his Machiavellian cunning and organisational genius had taken him to the pinnacle of the underworld heirarchy.

He also had much of Tammany Hall, the city's political fulcrum, under his control. One palm that he bountifully greased was that of James J. Hines, the politically quixotic Democratic leader of the Eleventh Assembly District and a major mover and shaker in the Upper West Side. In return for the generous contributions he received towards his election campaigns, Hines provided Schultz with the protective umbrella of his considerable political fiefdom, in which the Dutchman's illicit empire could prosper. With shrewd presence of mind, Schultz tilted the balance of power to such an extent that the thug was now the boss and the political mandarin his stooge. He practised total control: all officials were bribed according to their rank, and all elections were rigged. Though violent by nature, he believed that the bribe was mightier than the bullet in this instance.

Such was the web of corruption woven by Tammany Hall that future Mayor of New York Fiorella La Guardia was prompted to observe that it would take a police force of at least a quarter of a million officers to enforce Prohibition and a further quarter of a million people to police the police.

*

The years Coll spent in custody saw America go on an unprecedented buying spree. Millions of people bought stocks on margin – no cash up front – hoping that the accrued profit would pay for the shares. The country was optimistic and it looked as though the economic boom would never end. But end it did, with a crash. Black Friday 1929 marked the beginning of the worst depression the world has ever seen. More than 16 million shares changed hands, as their value plummeted by 40 per cent in just a few hours. The ecomomic ramifications of the crash spread throughout the country. As the roaring twenties petered to a whimper, thousands of factories shut their gates and entire families were forced to camp in makeshift hobo cities, as dust storms swept across the American Midwest like an apocalyptic plague. Urban legend had it that when a person booked a room in a New York hotel they would be asked by the receptionist if they wanted to sleep in it or jump from one of its windows!

Despite the economic malaise, the mob had never had it so good. Consumption of liquor continued unabated as people drank to forget the humdrum misery of their lives. Indeed the demand for alcohol far exceeded the supply. Similarly, illegal gambling fed the false promise of immense wealth, while some women turned to prostitution simply to survive. Gangsters controlled all of these rackets, establishing a monopoly in supplying the masses with the opiate of their choice.

Small wonder then that a young criminal like Vincent Coll, emerging from prison with few or no qualifications save the graduate workshops in advanced felony that Elmira had offered, chose to pursue a career of crime. It must have been difficult for a man of Coll's temperament to accept that on his release from detention he would have to hitch his wagon to Schultz's star if he was to avoid going down the conventional route of looking in the 'situations vacant' columns of newspapers. There was also the small matter of regaining Schultz's confidence after having ostracised him as a child. The last few years had seen a massive reversal in their fortunes. It was always unlikely, though, that Coll would settle for a menial position as a hired hand, so he had to persuade the Dutchman that his skills in extortion were indispensible.

All that remained now were the logistics of how, when and where. Legend has it that, less than a week after his release from Elmira, Coll strutted into Schultz's headquarters in Joe Noe's first speakeasy on Brook Avenue. He stood at the bar, where he had a fine view of his childhood foe. Schultz, he observed, had changed little, except for the fact that his deficiency in the personality stakes was even more pronounced than it had been before. His social awkwardness was now ballasted by power, wealth and influence, however. Nobody in his right mind would dare challenge the Dutchman on his own territory.

Sitting at Schultz's table was a great beast of a man with carefully sculpted black hair and a taut, puggish look. He was Abe 'Bo' Weinberg, the Mike Tyson of the underworld. A well-endowed, peroxide blonde, her face caked in warpaint, completed the triumvirate. Her name was Millie Slobodnick, but as soon as she had left her native place, a small Pennsylvanian mining town, she operated under the stage name of Trixie Tralee. Coll could see that Trixie was bored silly. Schultz was on a big power trip and was basking in ego-tickling adulation. But all of the Dutchman's money could not buy Coll's panache or sexual allure. Vincent seized the opportunity by giving the broad the eye, and within minutes she had ambled casually over to where he was standing. Vincent went on a charm offensive. A drink was proffered and Trixie was immediately enraptured by Coll's amusing line of flattery. Schultz felt of stab of jealousy. He threw Coll a withering glance. Who was this tall, russet stranger who had dared to make advances on his moll in his own backyard?

Never noted for his arbitration skills, Schultz sent the simian Weinberg over to sort out his amatory rival. Coll had expected as much, so when Bo grabbed him by the shoulder and spun him around he was met with a left hook on the chin. This was followed by a quick right and a knee in the groin, and within minutes Bo Weinberg, the most feared hard man in New York, lay flat on his back. Coll ordered two more drinks and slapped a big, moist kiss on Trixie's lips. Everything had gone to plan. Schultz invited Coll to join him at his table for a drink. Vincent was in no mood to leave his new-found friend's sprightly company, though, and gave her one last public show of affection. Both men instantly recognised each other, with Schultz basking in the glory of hammering home the fact that he was now the big shot on the block. He had a proposition for Vince. He admired his effrontery in taking on Weinberg and coming out unscathed. Tough guys with moxie weren't easily come by, and Coll's pluck and self-confidence could prove invaluable to Schultz's business. In return for his allegiance, Coll would be made a salesman in the Schultz operation. He would be assigned a regular beat, where he would control the speakeasies and bootleggers as well as book orders. He'd be expected to keep current customers on board and persuade others of the merits of opening an account with the Schultz organisation. A deal was struck, and Coll was to receive $75 a week, plus commission, for his services, with the understanding that his salary would rise to $100 if he proved his worth. He would bring his older brother, Peter, into the fold as well.

Coll's humiliation of Weinberg was a pyrrhic victory. Shorn of his dignity, big Bo harboured a deep-seated resentment of the Gaoth Dobhair man from that day forth. Weinberg is suspected of having been the person who deposited those final fifteen slugs in the telephone booth in the New London Pharmacy. In the classic opening scene of the movie *Billy Bathgate*, Weinberg, played by Bruce Willis, confesses to the killing of Coll as the cement hardens around his feet in preparation for his date with the fishes in the tumbling East River. Schultz's loyal lieutenant had overstepped the mark by talking to Lucky Luciano about his boss's future. He was unhappy about the fact that the proceeds of the policy rackets were being drained off to foot Schultz's ever-increasing legal bills.

What happened next was subsequently revealed in 1962 during the sensational US Senate hearings into the workings of organised crime by Maranzano's bodyguard and chauffeur, Joe Valachi, the most celebrated canary in history. On 9 September 1935, Bo's showgirl wife, Anna May Turner, reported her husband's absence after he failed to turn up for his dinner. 'He must be dead, for nothing would keep him from coming to see me or letting me know where he is,' she declared. The story on the grapevine was that Schultz had personally executed him and dumped the body into a cement-mixer in Cementon, New York.

That Coll proved his worth to the Dutchman is more a testimony of his moral bankruptcy than of any great business acumen. He displayed only wisps of astuteness. Extortion and blackmail seem to have been the main weapons in his armoury and his powers of persuasion soon translated into brisk business. One of the most horrific acts attributed to him, which occurred during his period on Schultz's payroll, was the subjugation of the Rock brothers. John and Joe Rock were Irish bootleggers who had a well-established foothold in the Bronx when Arthur and Vince were still in short trousers. John was persuaded by Coll to stand aside, but his more stubborn brother refused to play ball. It fell upon Vincent to make him see sense.

It is often suggested that Coll lost the run of himself after the death of his brother Peter, but the sordid details of the torture he inflicted upon Joe Rock effectively punctures this myth. It suggests that a sick, sadistic mind had already been at work at a much earlier age.

Coll had Rock kidnapped and beaten to a pulp. He hung him on a meat hook by the thumbs and blindfolded him with a strip of gauze that had been soaked in a mixture that contained the drippings of a gonorrhoeal infection. Rock's family had to muster up a ransom of $35,000 for the return of his bludgeoned body. He retired from trading a blind and broken man.

Joe Rock's round trip to hell was Coll's first foray into the world of mob kidnapping, a sphere of criminality with which he had become synonymous by the time of his death.

4

Dog Eat Dog

Coll's marriage of convenience with the Dutchman was never likely to go the distance. It was inevitable that two such volatile egos would collide sooner or later. Coll was something of a hellraiser and nonconformist free spirit; he would not tolerate any restriction of his horizons. Schultz, on the other hand, was a figure of blazing contradictions, holding violently contrary opinions simultaneously. Though Coll's effectiveness as a cold-blooded gunman was not in question, his overt manifestations of mutiny and his resentment of taking orders were spiralling out of control.

Relations between the two men first became strained in the wake of the daring Sheffield Farm robbery, which Coll carried out with the aid of another old neighbour, Carmine Barelli. Coll and Barelli disguised themselves as the security guards of the armoured truck that came around to the main Bronx office at 166th and Webster Avenue once a week to pick up the payroll. The cashier promptly handed over the sack of cash; the two young gangsters had netted the tidy sum of $18,000 in the space of two minutes. It was an audacious, brilliantly orchestrated raid – a reputation-enhancing master stroke that indicates Coll's savvy despite his baby face.

Dividing the spoils from the Sheffield Farm job proved problematic, however. The heist had been masterminded by Coll, who had even sourced the uniforms; all Barelli had had to do was turn up and pocket the loot. This was not lost upon Vince, who refused a 50-50 split. Barelli sought the intervention of Schultz, who viewed the whole incident as an act of insubordination and demanded his own piece of the pie. The final settlement saw Coll and Barelli get $6,000 each, while the same amount went into one of Schultz's 'sinking funds'. All told, this was a pretty poor return for all the energy and cunning that Vincent had expended.

The life of a hired hand was never likely to sit easily on the shoulders of Coll, whose leadership qualities were beyond doubt. He was earning $150 a week at the time, a mere pittance for a man of his tastes. By that stage, Schultz's partner, Joey Noe, had departed the scene, slain amid a hail of bullets by a lone gunman believed to be in the employ of Legs Diamond. Coll saw himself as Noe's natural successor and suggested as much to the Dutchman. According to information in the files of the Manhattan District Attorney's Office, Coll demanded his own piece of the beer trade in the Bronx and Harlem. Never noted for his largesse, Schultz was not amused at the suggestion that he should relinquish some of his power to one of his hirelings. He had coped adequately on his own following the death of Noe and was not interested in carving up his manorial rights. He issued Coll with a curt refusal.

It was at this stage that Coll decided to go it alone. In his eyes, the economics were simple: it cost $3 to $4 to manufacture a keg of the brew that fetched $8 to $9 from the distributors and $18 to $19 in the speakeasies. There was a lot of money to be made from illegal booze during the Prohibition and one man appeared to have a monopoly on the entire New York market.

Headstrong and ambitious, Coll decided to set up a rival gang, against all sane judgement, with the hope of making significant inroads into Schultz's snowballing wealth; Schultz was reckoned to be earning up to $20 million a year. Coll's scheme was a Herculean undertaking by any standards and was in effect the first significant challenge to Schultz's iron grip on organised crime, which Coll himself had been so instrumental in consolidating.

Relations between the two men had been festering for some time and the idea of a split had apparently been gestating quietly in Coll's mind for a number of months. This was deemed to be the right time to break away. He set up camp half a block away from Schultz's headquarters on Brook Avenue and started to recruit from within his old employer's ranks. Some discordant notes had been re-sounding in the Schultz camp of late, and Coll took with him some of the Dutchman's most proficient hired hands. These included his brother Pete, Frank Giordano, Dominic 'Tuffy' Odierno, Arthur Palumbo and one of the most feared assassins in the underworld, Edward Popke, also known as 'Fats McCarthy' or 'John the Polack'.

One man Coll failed to tempt away, however, was Carmine Barelli. Although relations between the two had soured considerably since the Sheffield Farm dust-up, Coll was aware that Barelli was a vital cog in the Schultz operation. He was one of Schultz's most loyal lieutenants and had many contacts with rum-runners who sailed down from Canada to set up better liquor distribution.

After several rebuffs, tensions were further fuelled when Barelli was the first to inform Schultz of the imminent revolt. He was flirting with disaster. Raising the hackles of someone as morally delinquent as Vincent Coll could only lead to tragedy. With Coll there was never likely to be an appeals process.

Coll bided his time and hatched a simple plan for revenge. It centred on Barelli's Achilles heel – his girlfriend, May Smith, an old acquaintance of Vincent. Born May Kartzmasky in the small town of Catasanqua, Pennsylvania, she was a naive young dance hostess who thought no ill of anyone, least of all her old friend. Described in contemporary accounts as a 'cute broad', May was twenty-two years old and had recently divorced. She was extremely innocent and totally out of her depth in the company she kept. In recent weeks she had remained on good terms with Coll even though there was obviously no love lost between him and her boyfriend.

One night as she made her way to her home on Wythe Place, May was accosted by Coll. In the banter that ensued, Coll spouted the usual platitudes until he had put Smith completely at her ease. Eventually the subject of Barelli was broached, with Coll expressing regret that their long-standing friendship had been so abruptly terminated. He told her that he wanted to bury the hatchet and reforge their friendship but that this was impossible because Barelli refused to meet him. He asked, with a spark of mischief, whether she would be willing to help him bump into her boyfriend 'accidentally on purpose'. Smith too regretted that two such 'swell' guys should have fallen out and said that she would arrange for Barelli to escort her home at 2 am the following night. Coll would wait in his car until they arrived and would 'unintentionally' bump into them at 170th Street and Inwood Avenue.

At 2.12 am on 13 February 1930, a car containing Vincent Coll, Frank Esposito and the clown-faced Patsy del Greco pulled up on the sidewalk as the young couple made their way homewards.

'Hello there, Carmine,' Coll called agreeably. A look of terror flitted across Barelli's face. The impending doom had not apparently registered with May Smith, however, who greeted Vincent with her usual affability. Three slugs later, Barelli's body lay limp on the ground, blood trickling from his mouth and congealing on the icy pavement. Smith was horror-stricken and numb with dread. Her eyes glazed with tears. But her entreaties were to no avail. Coll's face splintered into a reluctant smile.

'Baby, I'm awful sorry,' he was reported to have said, with a finality that left no hope for appeal, 'but you seen it, so you gotta go too.'

May Smith's death certificate registers her cause of death as a haemorrhage caused by a 'bullet wound of chest, neck and head penetrating lung, trachea and brain'. She was buried back home in Pennsylvania after a quiet family funeral – a sad end to a largely innocuous life.

Barelli's removal seems to have been a more raucous affair, however, if the following anecdote from Victor Rosen's *Dark Plunder* is anything to go by. To allay suspicions, Vince had gone to pay his respects to his victim's mother:

> So Vince went to see Mrs Barelli and told her how
> sorry he was about what happened, what a great guy

Carmine was and how much he loved him.

She made a big fuss over him, too. *Sí, sí*, he had indeed been her son's good friend. Carmine loved Vincenzo like a brother. She asked him if he'd like to have a last look at him.

He didn't want to, but he knew it was expected so he'd better do that, too. She took him into the front parlour, where they had Barelli laid out in his fancy clothes in a fancy box with flowers piled on it and a seven-foot gate made out of white carnations with a ribbon that said, 'Gone, But Not Forgotten, Old Pal. From Dutch and His Boys.'

Vince knew what to do when he got in there. He knelt by the casket, crossed himself, mumbled a prayer, crossed himself again and got up. Now he looked inside the coffin.

Barelli's face was neat and peaceful enough. They'd done a good job of patching up the holes in his head. In fact, he looked kind of happy and contented. With his right hand he was thumbing his nose!

Mrs Barelli had been wailing and sobbing, but now she stopped. She was looking straight at Coll, watching him. There was a crooked smile on her lips too.

'My Carmine, he ask me to bury him so,' she said. 'You wanna know why, Vincenzo?' Vince didn't want to know, but she went on just the same. 'One night lasta week he come home. He look like he is sick, or in trouble or in love.

"No, no, *mamma mia*," he say. But I got eyes in the head and some things a mamma do not have to see.

Finalemente he tella me what it is that bother him and you know what he say, Vincenzo?' Her eyes narrowed as she peered at him across the open casket. 'He tella me, "*Mamma mia,* I gotta funny feelin', here inside. I think maybe I gonna die very soon." *Dio mio!* I cross myself and say he musta not speak such things, it is *molto, molto cattivo,* very bad. But he say no, I should not be afraid because some day we all gotta die and he no have the fear to die. But one thing only he ask me I should do for him and he make me swear I do it. "If maybe in the next coupla days they bring me home dead, do not cry for me too much," he say. "But this one thing I wanna you should do for me – put me in the casket *cosí,* with the fingers at the nose. My frien', Vincenzo, he will come to see you to tella you how much he love me, how much he was my frien', and then when he tella you that, *mamma mia,* I want that you should take him into the *salone* and make him look at me with the fingers at the nose and then," my Carmine say, "and then – " Her eyes opened wide. The veils dropped from them and they burned with a fierce, relentless hate.

'" – and then, *mamma mia,* you will know that Vincenzo, my very old, dear frien', who love me so very much – he is the one who kill me!"'

She stopped.

The silence was a living thing. Vince could feel it throbbing and beating against his brain.

Now the old woman moved slowly, majestically towards the coffin. She bent down. With tenderness and grace she kissed her son's cold lips. Then she brought his hand down, gently, and folded it over the other hand and placed a crucifix between them. She crossed herself.

Vince watched in a kind of a trance. He crossed himself quickly. Then he fled.

As an addendum to Rosen's yarn, Cáit Nic Giolla Bhríde's summation of the Coll family's most striking physical feature springs to mind: '*Bhí gaosán fada ag na Tuathaill uilig!*' ('All Toaly's family had long noses.')

Vincent Coll was never charged with the double killing.

*

Barelli's murder should probably be viewed in isolation as an act of vengeance and a squaring of a personal vendetta rather than as the opening gambit of the gangland blood-letting that followed. In slaying one of Schultz's most loyal deputies, however, Coll had clearly signalled his intentions.

Schultz's beer trucks began to disappear on an alarmingly regular basis, and the owners of speakeasies serviced by his empire were intimidated and persuaded to switch their allegiances to Coll. Vincent also started to muscle in on Schultz's numbers rackets. Though hopelessly outnumbered, the young tearaway openly boasted that his objective was to wipe out the Dutchman's $20-million-a-year empire. To many, this would seem to suggest that Coll was a few verses short of a Koran. It is a measure of the fear which Coll had instilled in his fellow mobsters, however, that Schultz's biographer, Paul Sann, who was the *New York Post*'s executive editor for twenty-nine years, makes out in his book *Kill the*

Dutchman that Coll brought more trouble upon the Dutch-man than the entire New York Police Department:

> the brash Mick . . . caused his old buddy more damn
> trouble than anybody but the paid assassin who put
> that last slug into his side. There was just no way to
> deal with Vincent Coll except by force; you could not
> set up a peace conference with him no matter how
> soft you made the terms.

Though no shots had as yet been fired in anger, both sides were shaping up for a showdown. Coll must have had a fine opinion of his own worth, for he had no more than ten people working for him. With the exception of his brother Peter and the Pole Fats McCarthy, most of his gang were of Italian extraction. Many of them were defectors from the Schultz camp. They read like the dramatis personae of a Damon Runyon book. The designated driver was Frank Giordano, a blade-faced, spindly man with sharp, ferrety features. Giordano, who was known as 'back-knifer', was to die in the electric chair in less than two years' time, along with another member of the gang, Dominic Odierno. Though not the brightest boy on the block, the chicken-necked and pigeon-chested Tuffy Odierno was a popular figure amongst the gangster fraternity, to the extent that his former boss, Dutch Schultz, kept him in cigarettes during his final months on death row even though he had been convicted of murdering one of Schultz's own right-hand men. Another defector was the lank-haired Michael 'Mike Oach' Basile. The slovenly Pasquele Del Greco, whose face was like a permanent tear, was one of the few gang members who had served time. Vincent 'Jimmie' di Lucia, Frank Palumbo and Frank Facchaino were also Coll retainers.

The degree of the inconvenience and vexation that Coll caused the Dutchman can be measured by a tale that a famous Bronx detective, Fred Schaedel, used to tell. A rambling raconteur, Schaedel remembered both Coll and Schultz from their childhood days as two of the toughs who used to terrorise him when he had to escort his little sister home from piano lessons. At the onset of the Coll-Schultz feud, Schaedel was working in the Morrisania Police Precinct in the Bronx, which is now a sleepy storage area set in a sylvan hollow, hugged on all sides by spiralling motor junctions. Some time at the beginning of 1931, Schultz walked into the precinct and approached three detectives in the squad room. Fred Schaedel was one of the detectives. The Dutchman didn't beat around the bush.

'Look, I want the Mick killed. He's driving me out of my mind,' Schultz declared. 'I'll give a house in Westchester to any of you guys who knocks him off.'

Westchester was an affluent, leafy suburb of New York, a place where someone on a detective's salary could hardly aspire to live.

'Arthur, do you know what you're saying?' Schaedel reminded him. 'Do you know that you're in the Morrisania Station?'

'I know where I am,' the Bronx Beer Baron growled. 'I've been here before. I just came in to tell you that I'll pay good to any cop who kills the Mick!'

When Schultz was asked to elaborate, he baldly pronounced, 'The guy that kills the Mick gets the Honour Medal anyway – I'm just makin' it more interesting.'

This murder contract, verbally delivered to three NYPD detectives, was a brazenly overt display of corruption, and it is a measure of the power that the crime kings wielded that Schultz was never brought to book for it. It was also symptomatic of the impotency of the entire legal system of the era. Had he been charged, the case would in all likelihood have been thrown out of court as a poor attempt at humour by a judge who would undoubtedly have been on the Schultz payroll.

'We never could have made it stick,' Schaedel confided to the journalist Paul Sann forty years later. 'The Dutchman would have walked out five minutes after his lawyer arrived. He'd just say he was kiddin' with us. Besides, it was a good bet by then that Schultz and the Mick were going to take care of each other, one or the other, without our help. We had our hands full just picking up the bodies they were scattering around the borough in those days.'

Schaedel was referring to the carnage visited on New York in the summer of 1931. The moral pollution of Chicago had now come to the Big Apple, courtesy of Coll and Schultz. Tommy-guns blazed and gangsters fell as hostilities between the two former colleagues worsened. The final death count and casualty list in the Coll-Schultz conflict may never be determined, as most of those who perished were mere foot soldiers or manual labourers in the beer-drops that Coll put under siege. Though the metropolitan dailies bandied about outrageous ballpark figures of forty or fifty, the final toll probably amounted to about ninteen, including those executed by the state.

First to go was a man who may not have belonged to either camp and whose only crime was that he bore an uncanny resemblance to Vincent Coll. The Mad Dot Boat Club was a speakeasy at 251 Dyckman Street owned jointly by Jimmie De Lucia, an associate of Coll's, and his sister Mrs Anna Elario. Some months previously, Coll had cut himself in as a partner to the Lilliputian De Lucia without prompting a whimper of protest from De Lucia; he offered protection and a constant supply of cheap liquor. Coll ran a mean business. One night, for example, he took an immediate dislike to one of his customers and ordered him to leave. The man casually informed him that he would do so as soon as he had finished his beer. Coll grabbed the bottle in an apoplectic rage, smashed it on the counter and thrust its serrated edge into the stranger's face. 'Now,' he snarled, 'your beer is finished. Get out!'

The club was a favourite hang-out of Coll's and an obvious target for Schultz's henchmen. On 12 May, they laid down a stream of fire in front of the club and did not linger long enough in enemy territory to discover that they had bumped off the wrong man. The man who was killed was in fact Roy Herbert Sloane, the handsome boy prodigy who had argued his way out of Sing Sing. Of all the gin joints in all the world he had to walk into Coll's!

Known as 'College Boy Bandit', Sloane was a former undergraduate of Columbia University. His academic progress had been interrupted by a robbery rap and he studied law in prison with such success that he managed to secure his own release on appeal. Sloane and Coll were of much the same build and had many other physical characteristics in common. Sloane's assassins were convinced that they had trapped Coll, his underworld counterpart, when they opened fire outside the favourite rendezvous of the twenty-three-year-old gang chieftain. It wasn't until October that the police made the connection, but the bush telegraph of the crime world relayed the news of the death squad's cock-up within minutes, and Schultz, who was petulant and aggressive at the best of times, was presumably not best pleased with his assassins' shoddy workmanship.

The police closed down the Mad Dot Club the day after Sloane was slain, and De Lucia moved to upstate New York, where he would renew acquaintances with Coll at a later date.

Six months later, the *New York Evening Post* raised the possibility that Sloane was in fact a member of the Coll gang. The *Post* claimed that Sloane operated as a front man for the gang. His suave appearance, excellent diction and poise enabled him to dispose of stocks and bonds and merchandise stolen by Coll's goons. On the night that he was slain, the youth had apparently spent his time looking for Vincent in his usual haunts in Brooklyn, the Bronx and Manhattan in the hope that the gang leader would pay him the $2,500 that he was due for 'a deal' that he had brokered with a tannery in New Jersey. Sloane, it appeared, had been dunning Coll for the money for some time. Whether or not he was a member of the gang is a matter of conjecture but there is no doubting the fact that he was not the intended target of the attack that killed him.

Hostilities soon escalated after Sloane's unfortunate death. On 29 May 1931 the *Post* reported that the beer battle between Harlem and Bronx hoodlums had 'assumed the proportions of a Chicago gangster war'. The Coll-Schultz feud, which had hitherto consisted principally of threats and beer-truck hijacking, had flared up the previous night, when a machine-gun 'chopper', crouched in a large sedan with drawn curtains, rattled a murderous fire on Dominic Bologna, a Bronx beer salesman, and Frank 'Big Dick' Amato as they stood in front of 164 East 116th Street talking to the Harlem racketeer Joe Rao. The three men were conversing quietly when the sedan slowed down in front of them. Amato and Bologna attempted to break away from Rao, but before they could move, the chopper began pouring a leaden stream on them. They staggered towards a parked car but one of the four men in the sedan jumped out and fired four shots from a revolver. All four shots were on target, and the sedan and its occupants sped away. Both Amato and Bologna were euphemistically described on their death certificates as salesmen. Rao was wounded in the raid and fled the scene of the crime immediately. The police suspected at the time that he may have been kidnapped, but this proved to be unfounded.

The shootings had a certain degree of novelty value at the time, and more than 2,000 curious bystanders were attracted by the excitement. Police reserves from the East Sixty-seventh Street Precinct were rushed to the scene to keep order. Unaware of the feud between the Mick and the Dutchman, police attributed the double murders to an effort to assassinate Rao, who they suspected had been invading the beer territory controlled by Dutch Schultz in the Bronx. Rao was a close associate of Ciro Terranova, 'the Artichoke King' – so called because he had established a monopoly on the wholesale trade in that particular commodity, which was an essential part of the staple diet of all Italians. Police Commissioner Mulrooney ordered that Schultz be taken in for questioning immediately.

The police department's intelligence was way off the

mark, however, as Terranova and Rao had recently aligned themselves with the Dutchman to form an *entente cordiale* of sorts.

The reprisal was as swift as it was inevitable. In targeting Peter Coll, Vincent's senior by a year and four months, Schultz hit the Mick where it hurt most. Peter had lived under the constant shadow of his more handsome younger brother. He had a puggish look, with an outscrolled underlip set in a bulbous face. His blemished skin and wheatish complexion made him look a good deal older than Vincent. He had deeply socketed bird-of-prey eyes, an aggressive chin and a mouth like a bruised frog. His eyes were almost without colour, reflecting neither interest nor intelligence.

Both brothers' lives had been based on the same template. They had always looked out for one another while under the guardianship of their aunt Mary Friel – and especially during their teenage detention in the Catholic Protectory. The intimacy of their relationship went beyond the usual attachment of siblings, possibly stemming from the fact that they had been left parentless at a very young age. Peter was Vincent's aide and confidant and was always on hand for him when required. Reserved and introverted, he had a stabilising influence on his hell-raising brother. Though a lightweight in the underworld and a mere footnote in the hall of infamy, he in fact had a more crowded criminal record than his kid brother. He was charged in the District Court in the Southern District of New York on 14 June 1930 with unlawful possession of a gallon of anisette and a pint of whiskey. He failed to appear, however. His bail bond was forfeited and a bench warrant was ordered. When he eventually turned up in court, on 8 December, he pleaded guilty and was fined $25. A graver transgression occurred in April 1931, when he was arrested in a Broadway apartment on the strength of a police tip-off that he intended to put a rival gangster 'on the spot'. He was carrying a gun at the time and was awaiting trial for violation of the Sullivan Law, having been released on $2,500 bail on 21 April. He never lived to stand trial.

On the morning of 30 May 1931, Peter Coll was shot in a Harlem street while on his way home to his house on 2201 Marion Avenue, the Bronx. As he drove down St Nicholas Street, near 111th Street, in Tuffy Odierno's car, another vehicle, containing four men, drew up alongside him. Four shots were fired through the windshield; Peter was struck by all of them. He swerved his car in an attempt to get away but crashed into a wall. His death certificate registers the chief and determining cause of death to have been a haemorrhage of his left chest from bullet wounds to his left back, left lungs and pulmonary veins. He was twenty-four years old.

Once again, the NYPD's appraisal of the situation was wide of the mark. They still had not twigged that a full-scale war between the rival Coll and Schultz gangs was now in progress. Vincent Coll had yet to be identified as a gang leader. His importance in the underworld had gone unnoticed by them; they dismissed him as a dealer in second-hand cars in Brooklyn and the proprietor of several third-rate speakeasies in the Bronx. Writing in the *Sunday News* that weekend, Louis Davidson reported that Peter had been tabbed by the police as a Schultz henchman. Commissioner Mulrooney's finger of suspicion again pointed at the Artichoke King and, fearing further reprisals, he deployed a special detail of a hundred men in Bronx hot spots over the Whit weekend.

Vincent was devastated by his brother's death and vowed to get even. Whether or not Coll's transmogrification from a footloose racketeer into a reckless psychopath can be attributed to his brother's assassination cannot easily be determined. The event was clearly a personal watershed, however. Though his madcap lunge for revenge was un- doubtedly bolstered by his sense of loss, some presaging signs had earlier emerged. Extenuating circumstances not- withstanding, the torture of Joe Rock and the cold-blooded slaying of Barelli and Smith would suggest that the rot had set in a good deal earlier. What we can be sure of, however, was that he took Peter's fatal shooting very badly, to the extent that it retarded his outlook. It triggered something in him and severed the thin emotional thread that he had been hanging on to. It was also the catalyst for a new spate of bloodletting.

His response was immediate and brutal. Just after two o'clock on the morning of 31 May, hours after Peter had been killed, three men shot Gennaro 'Chin' Atari, a Schultz collector, while bowling in an alley at 354 East 149th Street. Atari's body was found beside some benches in front of the alleys. Though the killers were never identified, there can be little doubt that it was the work of the Coll gang.

Two days later, in a scene reminiscent of a James Cagney movie, two sedans belonging to the rival gangs had a rip- roaring shoot-out on 177th Street. Onlookers rushed for cover as the cars took off down the street side by side at high speed, firing indiscriminately at each other. Remarkably, only Patsy del Greco, of the Coll gang, was injured – a gunshot wound to the arm – while all of the Schultz contingent and the innocent bystanders who watched the sideshow emerged unscathed. Later that evening Coll led a raid on a Schultz garage and forced the workers to demolish twenty brand new trucks, along with 150 slot machines.

Just before 5 am the following morning, the body of Louis de Rosa, a close associate of the Dutchman, was found at Rider Avenue and 137th Street with five bullet wounds to his head. The same number of bullets was used to kill John Jacapraro, one of Schultz's truck drivers, whose body was found in an abandoned Buick at 1347 Stratford Avenue on 8 June.

On Bloomsday of that year, Abe Rosenberg, another acolyte of Schultz's, was taken for a ride from which there was no return. His bludgeoned body was found in Black Swamp Road, Queens. His death certificate lists a gunshot wound to the head as the cause of death.

The police had so far adopted a laissez-faire attitude to the feud, evidently believing it to be self-regulating. To ward off any escalation in hostilities, however, the NYPD found themselves keeping an eye on the Dutchman's beer-drops. Fred Schaedel and his partner, for example, were assigned to stake out one of Schultz's largest plants on Randall Avenue, in the Hunt's Point section of the Bronx, in an unmarked car. Schultz's men recognised them from the outset and could not have been more courteous to them. Any form of protection, even from the cops, was to be welcomed at that stage of the hostilities.

It was clear that Coll, who was behaving like a raging bull, was not in complete control of his faculties and was capable of doing anything. He would have been regarded as a card-carrying psychopath – if he could only simmer down a bit. No one understood this more than the Dutchman.

The extent to which the Mick had downsized his once-bloated operation in the space of a few days prompted Schultz to run to ground. He lived in mortal fear of reprisals as he holed up in an elegant ninth-floor apartment at 1212 Fifth Avenue under the assumed name of 'Russell Jones'. His room, which had a view of Central Park, cost the Dutchman a mere $2,500 per annum. The elementary-school drop-out spent his time there catching up on Dickens, American history and some medical journals. An obsessive neurotic, Schultz was reported to be keeping sober so that he could be perpetually on the alert. When he was eventually apprehended several months later, Coll laughed like a drain as he rasped maliciously, 'Well, I suppose he's drunk now for the first time in weeks.'

That Coll had instilled the fear of God into the Dutchman is an understatement. On the evening of 18 June, Schultz and his bodyguard, 'Dangerous' Dan Iamascia, were dropped home by their new-found ally, the Artichoke King, after a particularly cordial policy conference. Having disgorged its load, Terranova's armour-plated sedan took off down Fifth Avenue at a great clip. As he ambled towards his apartment, Schultz spotted two figures lurking in the shadows. Assuming they belonged to a Coll death squad, he reached for his gun but was beaten to the draw by his adversaries. Shots rang out in the inky blackness, and when the smoke had cleared Iamascia lay on the sidewalk spuming blood. Schultz threw his revolver in the gutter and took to his heels. He was not fast enough, though, as the towering torso of Steve di Rosa bore down on him and knocked him to the ground. The Dutchman's assailant was not in fact a member of the Coll gang but a police detective. Along with his colleague, Detective Julius Salke, di Rosa had been staking out the apartment of 'Russell Jones' since early that morning following a tip-off from a female caller that had revealed the true identity of the suite's occupant.

Schultz's face instantly registered relief when he caught the glint of an NYPD badge.

'Jesus, am I glad you're cops!' he blurted, his body slowly untensing. 'For a minute I thought you was the opposition, out to gimme the works.'

Assuaged by the knowledge that his temporal visa had not as yet expired, the Dutchman reverted to his favourite defence mechanism: he thrust his hand into his pocket and withdrew a wad of loose change that amounted to the tidy sum of $18,645.

'Here, take it all!' Schultz pleaded.

As baksheesh inducements go, it wasn't bad, but di Rosa would have none of it. When his colleague caught up with him, he had to wrench di Rosa from the Dutchman, as he was in the process of shoving the roll of banknotes down the gangster's throat.

The two cops dropped Iamascia off at Mount Sinai Hospital, where he passed away a few hours later. He was later buried amid great pomp and ceremony in St Raymond's Cemetery in the Bronx, a few rows away from where Coll would soon take up residence.

Having safely disposed of Iamascia, the agents took his boss to the 104th Street Station House, where he was charged with felonious assault and violation of the Sullivan Law. Undeterred by his earlier encounter with di Rosa, Schultz upped the ante to $50,000 apiece, as well as the much-coveted houses in Westchester. Once again, his boodle failed to tempt the two upright detectives.

Bail was set at $75,000 for all counts, as the Dutchman faced a possible twenty years in jail. The case was heard by Judge Corrigan – a notoriously severe judge who would soon become well acquainted with Coll – in a heavily fortified General Sessions courtroom. The police had received information that Coll planned to assassinate the Dutchman during the trial. He would rather see Schultz dead than linger in prison. Forty heavily armed detectives and ten uniformed patrolmen guarded the courthouse to avert any such threat. All of the detectives had been chosen by Assistant Chief Inspector Sullivan because they had come in contact with Coll at some time or other in the past in arrests for which he was never convicted of a serious offence. That the police took the report seriously was indicated by their vigilance in questioning visitors to the courthouse at the various entrances at Centre, Lafayette, White and Leonard Streets. In addition, they searched all cars parked in the vicinity. The detectives were instructed not to admit any suspect until satisfied that his visit was in no way connected with the presence of Schultz. When in doubt, the detectives followed individuals to the courts in which they said they had business and remained there until satisfied by attachés that their visits were legitimate. Many of the detectives who patrolled the corridors were dressed as workmen. They used no elevators in their trips through the building and kept a constant eye on the stairways and dark corners of the massive structure to be sure that none of Coll's gang would escape their attention.

The *New York Times* reported that Schultz 'appeared to be the most nervous person in the courthouse. In the short time he was seated in court . . . the defendant kept sitting in his chair, nervously eyeing others present.'

It is a measure of Coll's steely and chilling determination that, although hopelessly outnumbered, he had reduced his rival to a gibbering bundle of nerves. When first arrested by Salke and di Rosa, the Dutchman had asked for a sedative to calm his frayed nerves. Once arraigned, he implored the police to protect his rights as a citizen and taxpayer by staving off the waiting press. The *Herald Tribune* portrayed him as 'a cringing, nerve-shattered individual who begged for a bromide sedative and was most fearful of a flashlight exposure.' Coll's campaign of terror was beginning to tell on him.

The Assistant District Attorney, John L. MacDonnell, used all this talk of Coll's order of execution to call Schultz's bluff. He asked the court to cancel the $75,000 bail on which Schultz had been at liberty since his indictment a fortnight previously and to lodge the defendant in the Tombs as a means of protecting him from Coll. Schultz's lawyer, David Goldstein, vociferously protested, stating that his client, having learned of Coll's death threat, had employed a private detective as a bodyguard. He called on the police for added protection.

Even as the first session of his trial drew to a close, Schultz was still terrified of Coll. He remained at the defence-counsel table until Judge Corrigan had agreed to continue his bail and court attachés had ordered everyone except his lawyer and private detective out of the room. Then he hesitantly started towards the door. When he saw some roughly dressed men, who happened to be detectives, there, he drew back. His lawyers and other detectives whispered assurances to him, and Schultz, surrounded by detectives and uniformed policemen, hurried down the stairs to a waiting cab. He had successfully survived Coll's death threat!

The Dutchman was eventually cleared of the assault charges and beat the Sullivan Law rap by virtue of the fact that he could produce a licence for the gun he had thrown in the gutter when di Rosa and Salke were hot on his heels. He had apparently obtained a permit some time previously by persuading a Suffolk County judge that he worked for the Belle Terrace Club in Long Island and that one of his duties involved transporting large sums of money for the owners of the club.

*

All was not quiet on the festering front, though. Predictably enough, there was no cessation of hostilities during the Dutchman's courtroom tribulations. Every self-respecting gangster knows that a knock on the door should be answered by a wife or girlfriend, as exemplified in the opening scene of *The Godfather Part 3*. On June 21 John Soricelli, another of Schultz's enforcers, violated this golden rule and for his troubles received two slugs in the chest from a pair of Coll henchmen. He staggered across the blood-dappled tiles to the kitchen and calmly asked his wife for a cigarette. When the police arrived they found him clutching his chest and blowing smoke rings. They interrogated him in the ambulance on his way to hospital but, even on death's door, he refused to break the underworld code of *omerta*. One breach of gangster etiquette was enough for one night. He was pronounced dead on arrival.

Soricelli was the ninth victim of the Coll-Schultz war, which had begun in earnest less than a month earlier. The narrow-gauge, backlash conservatism that had spawned Prohibition was coming home to roost: the metropolitan dailies were awash with the latest casualties of gangster bloodletting. Though the chronicle of gore was met with waves of revulsion and rhetoric, there was a feeling that the plateau of an unacceptable level of violence had not been reached. The danger was that the citizens of New York might become as inured to the daily diet of carnage as those of Chicago had before them. It was the announced determination of the two rival racketeers to shoot it out until one of them had established supremacy in the beer business uptown, and Peter Coll's assassination had only heightened and personalised the conflict. The stakes were high and the rules were clearly defined: this was a winner-take-all conflict and the possibility of stalemate did not enter the equation.

At this juncture, though, the Coll-Schultz feud had all the appearances of a battle to which only one side had turned up. Though the score now stood at 8-1 in favour of Coll, the odds were still stacked firmly against the Mick. Indeed, only three members of the central cell of Vince's core gang would survive to see another year – Jimmie De Lucia, a stool-pigeon who moved to the West Coast; Mike Basile, who received a life sentence in Dannemora Prison for shooting a detective; and Coll's latest recruit, his moll Lottie Kreisberger.

5

DOG IN HEAT

Advances made by the suffragette movement, coupled with Amelia Earhart's exploits in the field of aviation, saw a number of molls attain a position of authority in the gangster world – which is generally regarded as an all-men's club – in the late 1920s. One such woman was Lottie Coll. A brunette with depthless blue eyes, she can be seen in many ways as the gun-toting predecessor of Bonnie Parker.

In its 'Topics of the Times' column on 29 June 1933, the *New York Times* used Lottie Coll's indictment for manslaughter to editorialise on the important role played by the gangster's moll:

An indictment for murder [sic] has been found against the widow of a recently and suddenly removed gangster chieftain. It is a reminder that in few walks of life is there so much occupational comradeship between husband and wife as in the field of banditry.

The 'gun moll' is prominent in the strong-arm profession. She acts as a coadjutor in many ways. She is liaison officer, intelligence service, treasurer of the exchequer, diplomatic service. But if one may believe the best fictional literature on the subject, she is sometimes an actual participant in front-line operations. It is her business, with an eye to the Sullivan Law and the rules of evidence, to carry on her person the gun that may be requisitioned for duty at any moment. It is returned to her when the job is done.

When the enterprising gangster is a-gangstering, his capacity for sharing problems and ambitions with his wife is perhaps better than that of the average honest citizen.

This is as pithy a summation of Lottie's character and function as one is likely to find. Less a gangster's moll than a full-blown partner in crime, she was free-spirited and sharp-witted and exercised an almost Svengali-like dominance over her young boyfriend. She was more a neo-Depression mobster mastermind than a reluctant accomplice. Vincent Coll was like an unguided missile, while Lottie acted like a guidance system, manipulating him, often cynically, to accomplish her malignant motives.

An inveterate liar, Lottie's past was shrouded in secrecy. She looms large as a mystery figure in the underworld drama in which she was a central player. She was the Bermuda Triangle of the underworld. Men who were romantically linked to her simply vanished off the face of the earth or met with an ignominious end. She brought catastrophe to practically all of her lovers. Uncompromisingly thick-skinned and independent, she never let the men in her life get in the way of her self-serving cause. She was even more dangerous because she carried the implicit promise that she might eventually be tamed.

Born Charlotte von Denninger in Mannheim, Germany, she was the only daughter of Adelaide Whittler and Joseph von Denninger. The family emigrated to America while Lottie was still a baby and settled somewhere in the vicinity of Tenth Avenue. Her mother worked as a housemaid in the Bronx but died during Lottie's infancy. Her father was a professional gambler and allowed her great latitude in her social life. In her teenage years, she had become a familiar figure in the borough's dance halls. Even at a young age, she displayed fiendish predatory talents. In 1919 and 1920, while still in her early teens – it is never possible to be certain of her age – Lottie was arrested on burglary charges but was released on both occasions.

'Just call me Lottie,' she told reporters after Vincent had been slain. 'Kreisberger – the name by which I was known before I married Coll – was fictitious. I don't want to tell you what my real name was.'

'Kreisberger' was not in fact a fictitious sobriquet but the surname of her first husband, whom she married at the age of sixteen. Joe Kreisberger, a silk robber and petty thief, was married to her long enough to have sired a daughter, whose whereabouts or existence Lottie concealed from that day forth.

Lottie stuck with him briefly while the money rolled in from his burgeoning operations in the stolen-car insurance game, but her nocturnal activities were unsuited to domesticity. Shortly after marrying her, Joe disappeared, and he was never heard of again.

Far from being chastened by the experience, Lottie pursued her selfish goals with a singular purpose. Next up was Adolph Romano, a Harlem ice racketeer, in the pre-refrigeration era. Some suggest that Lottie divorced Joe Kreisberger before he vanished but there are no records available to substantiate this theory. Her new husband was to meet with a similar fate.

Lottie soon tired of Romano and began visiting night-clubs with various escorts. One such admirer was Sam Medal, an articulate, twenty-four-year-old Columbia College graduate. Needless to say, Romano was not best pleased and attempted to confront his amatory rival on the night of 7 July 1928 at Morris Avenue and 149th Street, the Bronx. Romano reached for a gun but was stabbed through the heart and died instantly.

Medal went to ground. The police sought him for months before he was, by chance, recognised in the subway by a detective. He stood trial in the Bronx later that year for Romano's murder but beat the rap on a legal technicality.

After his release Medal worked briefly as a bookmaker before opening a restaurant called Conté's at 147 West Forty-seventh Street, which was to become a favourite haunt of the Dutchman and other underworld luminaries. It was through this connection that Coll befriended Medal. Their flourishing friendship did not prevent Vincent from stealing the former's girlfriend. The $20,000 that Lottie inherited as a result of Romano's death would provide handy collateral to finance Coll's imminent split from Schultz. It is at this point that contemporary accounts report Medal as having vanished without trace.

This was not strictly true, however, as he in fact continued to work in the restaurant, possibly under an assumed name. His love for Lottie was only temporarily quenched and would resurface after Coll's telephone conversation was prematurely cut off in the spring of 1932. A report in the *New York Times* on 19 September 1932 proffered the opinion that Medal resumed his wooing of Coll's widow shortly after the Gaoth Dobhair man's death. We cannot be sure if his attentions were requited, but his wooing almost certainly accounted for his one-way ride in the autumn of 1932. Medal's courtship of Lottie connected him with two rival gangs – Schultz's and Coll's – and the police believed that one of the two had a part in his disappearance. Medal left his restaurant on the night of 6 September 1932 with $4,000 in cash. He was accompanied by two strangers. He had called his sister, with whom he lived in the Bronx, saying that business would detain him. The trio drove away in the lambent autumn night and Medal was never heard of again.

When exactly the fates of Vincent and Lottie collided is unclear. Four careening years in the federal penitentiary had stalled his testosterone and played havoc with his emotions. He had an outsize libido that had to be serviced. It was into this emotional cauldron that the vastly more experienced Lottie entered around 1931.

Heavy-set and big-boned, Lottie did not exactly fit the Prohibition-era fashion for svelteness. She possessed a wayward beauty, with flashing blue eyes, a steely stare and porcelain-pale skin. She had an indecipherable face framed by delicate cheekbones and a dewy complexion. Everything about her denoted presence.

Her high-octane self-assurance set Lottie apart from her peers. In many ways she was the classic old-school femme fatale – vacuous and vulnerable on the outside, calculating and relentless on the inside. She was, however, a mere prism through which the monumental shortcomings of the men around her were refracted. Lottie was a vamp who used her sexual attractiveness to seduce and feed off impressionable young men who had more hormones than sense.

She defied all stereotypes and challenged accepted gender roles. Gangsters' molls were by and large submissive and docile appendages, happy to benefit from their companions' ill-gotten gains without probing too deeply into the origins of these gains. The function of the moll is summed up extremely eloquently by Rich Cohen in *Tough Jews*:

> The women in the underworld were dolls, ornaments. Of course, they could sense the dread that surrounded their men, the menace the boys shed like light. Maybe it's what attracted them in the first place. But they had no idea how the boys earned that aura. Wives and girlfriends were insulated by many layers of ignorance. A man who tells his wife everything is a romantic, a fool. Ignorance protected the boys from the wives and the wives from the cops. If you know nothing, there is nothing to give away.

Lottie Kreisberger bucked this trend. As a career criminal she defied the social order. There is little to suggest that she was, to borrow a phrase from Hillary Clinton, a spineless lover, standing by her man like Tammy Wynette. Nor could she be described as a damsel in distress, out of her depth in traditionally masculine territory. Homely as apple pie one minute, *noir*-seductive the next, Lottie could manipulate men's desires while convincing them that the female psyche was something never to be fathomed.

Described by the *Daily News* as the brains behind the

Coll operation, Lottie had a pernicious influence on the impressionable young Gaoth Dobhair man. She was like a self-styled emotional actuary, filling the void left by Peter's murder. Known in the underworld as 'Queen Lottie', her shockproof, autocratic presence dominated those around her. She emerged from comparative obscurity as Coll's consort to a position of prominence in the underworld. It was Lottie's sense of cunning which was credited with transforming Coll, an ousted Schultz underling, into a leader of one of the most desperate gangs on the East Coast. Her briny confidence and brassy insolence were a perfect foil for Coll's vaulting ambition.

Vincent and Lottie proved to be an explosive couple. She had vision, will and cunning; he had power, charisma and an insatiable competitive streak. He was a tyrant of the mood swing: he could charm the paint off a gate one minute and empty a room the next. He could fly off the handle at the slightest provocation, while she was more temperate and duplicitous and could mould him like putty. There is no evidence to suggest, however, that Lottie ever tried to moderate the violence of his personality.

Though she was mercilessly mercenary, he worshipped the ground she trod on. She induced a weakness in him. Vincent Coll was a very complex and tormented personality who had great difficulties in coming to terms with the demands of life, and Lottie eased this burden for him. Their trust in each other was absolute. She took advantage of his servile devotion, though, and had a ruinous influence on him at an especially instructive time – when he required a partner who would counsel caution or, better still, bring his errant nature to heel.

Though Lottie claimed, in both newspaper interviews and in the filed affidavit for a marriage licence, to be no more than nine months older than Coll, the police believed that she may in fact have been seven years his senior. This would not be the first inconsistency in her stories – she also claimed to be a model who was never previously married! In the wake of Coll's murder, Lottie, aided by the consumption of the entire contents of a vial of aspirin, gave the *Daily Mirror* a powerful insight into the mechanics of her relationship with Vincent. Asked if she loved him, Lottie swallowed another three aspirins and sobbed, 'I'd certainly call it love!' Though her face was blotchy from crying, she managed to recover enough composure to launch into a defence of the dead gangster's character.

'If he had a dual nature, I never suspected it. These stories about his being so tough and a killer and all that – they didn't mean a thing to me. He was always a perfect gentleman with me.

'He never took me to nightclubs. We stayed at home and enjoyed home life. It was his practice to dine at home. He had the most marvellous personality for pleasing a woman.'

6

Dogs of War

Vincent Coll clearly could not pass an apple cart without wanting to upset it. The summer of 1931 saw him engaged in a thicket of mob dogfights which he had little chance of winning. He may have been bold, but his flagrant disregard for the gangland hierarchy clearly showed that he lacked the necessary nous to compete at a higher level.

The law of the jungle has little time for the hare-brained or foolhardy, and while the flamboyant Vincent Coll, Legs Diamond and Bugsy Siegel may have had their fifteen minutes of fame, their ostentatious behaviour drew attention to the underworld, and this attention in turn ultimately destroyed them. They were in effect public-relations bulimics, craving attention, gorging on it and throwing it back in society's face. It is imperative that those wishing to survive in the treacherous half-lit world of organised crime should avoid the limelight at all costs. So while Coll and his ilk flashed their tortured psyches like designer labels, shrewder mobsters who were in it for the long haul, like Lucky Luciano, Meyer Lansky, Owney Madden and Frank Costello, cloaked themselves in anonymity. Theirs was an altogether smoother style of malignity. They refused to be lured from the shadows into the glare, and their success was based on the diplomatic avoidance of violence. Bootleggers were most successful when they conformed closely to the methods of legitimate business and operated within clearly defined catchment areas. Coll, however, was less politically minded – and consequently less successful – than the new breed of Italian and Jewish gangster. He conformed to the Irish bootlegging stereotype, thinking in the short term and resorting to violent solutions. His harum-scarum, scatter-gun approach led to gang warfare, which made the public angry and forced the authorities to intervene. This upset the equilibrium of gangland, for bootleggers operated, by and large, with the tacit support of the man in the street.

While the new breed of gangster moved with great caution, Coll operated with reckless abandon. Bloated with his own importance, he was clearly ill-equipped to grapple with the rigours of the underworld pressure cooker. It was evident that he was unable to make the transition from terrorising rival small-time racketeers to rubbing shoulders with the bigwigs.

*

One such bigwig was Owney Madden, who was known affectionately as 'the Duke'. Coll misread his ducal reticence and shyness of publicity as a sign of vulnerability, for behind Madden's calm exterior was one the most powerful gangland supremos of the twentieth century. He was in fact the planet around which the satellites of Dutch Schultz, Lucky Luciano, Vannie Higgins and Waxey Gordon orbited. Though slight in stature, he was often referred to as 'Big Owney' in deference to the vastness of his operations. His standing in the underworld is best illustrated by a contemporary account in the *Police Gazette*:

This is the man who – from the standpoint of colour and excitement – towers over today's underworld figures the way Babe Ruth and Ty Cobb stand out above the ordinary ball players of this or any other era.

A small pretzel of a man, Madden had blue, larkish eyes, a corrugated neck and hands the size of lunch boxes. Born in Leeds in 1892, he was raised in Wigan before emigrating to America at the age of eleven. He always maintained a tinge of a Lancashire accent in his speech. Madden was a graduate of the Hell's Kitchen academy of criminals. On his arrival in America he lost no time in establishing his delinquent pedigree with the infamous Gopher Gang and was once described by an old sergeant at 'the Hell's Kitchen Precinct' as 'that little banty rooster from hell'. He rose to the rank of leader of the gang and by the age of twenty-three was suspected of having personally murdered five men. He particularly favoured the lead pipe as a weapon.

Madden had the reputation of being a serial womaniser – a penchant that very nearly led to his downfall. In full view of a dozen passengers, he shot a young clerk named William Henshaw on a trolley car as it rumbled up Ninth Avenue; he paused only to ring the conductor's bell. Henshaw's crime had been to take a shine to one of Madden's girlfriends and to have asked her out. Though Henshaw lived long enough to identify Owney as his attacker, the case collapsed because none of the witnesses were willing to come forward.

A rival gang, the Hudson Dusters, cornered Madden outside the Arbor Dance Hall on the night of 6 November 1912 and deposited eight slugs in him. While convalescing in hospital, he refused to break the underworld code of silence, telling the cops that his boys would take care of his assailants. He made one of the most-acclaimed comebacks since Lazarus; six of his would-be assassins died during his period of recuperation.

Another member of the Dusters, Patsy Doyle, suffered the humiliation of losing his moll, Freda Horner, to Owney. In response, Doyle informed the police of some of Madden's shady dealings and attacked one of his assistants. On 28 November 1914, Margaret Everdeane, a friend of Horner's, told Doyle that his former girlfriend wanted to meet up with him in order to bury the hatchet. When he arrived at the bar on Eighth Avenue, however, Horner was nowhere to be seen. Her friend, Margaret Everdeane, advised him to order a drink, as his former girlfriend would be along shortly. The barman then informed him that someone wanted to see him. That someone was Owney Madden, who pumped a single shot into his lung.

The Duke's lady friends were tracked down shortly afterwards, however, and they wilted under the pressures of severe police interrogation. Madden received twenty years in Sing Sing. When he was paroled nine years later, in 1923, he soon realised that the criminal landscape had altered considerably during his incarceration. The days of the Gophers and the Dusters were long gone. He emerged from prison a more refined and shrewder gangster, and after a brief period as a strike-breaker for a metropolitan cab company he proceeded to infiltrate the numbers rackets and the illegal liquor trade. He attained fame as the legendary proprietor of the Cotton Club, eternally immortalised in Francis Ford Coppola's big-budget 1985 movie of the same name. The Cotton Club was the most famous nightclub of the roaring twenties and is synonymous with the Jazz Age. It was patronised by such gangland luminaries as Lucky Luciano, Dutch Schultz and of course Mad Dog Coll, who liked to come down to Harlem to shoot the breeze. The greatest entertainers of the era, including Cab Calloway and Duke Ellington, performed in the Cotton Club in front of an all-white audience. Through his involvement with the club, Owney rubbed shoulders with the leading lights of American society. Known as 'the Duke of the West Side', he was a close personal friend of George Raft, Damon Runyon and President Batista of Cuba. Among his many lovers was Mae West, who described him as 'so sweet yet so vicious'.

*

One of the Duke's partners in crime was George Jean 'Big Frenchy' De Mange, the corpulent proprietor of the Club Argonaut on Seventh Avenue. Both men had teamed up as boxing promoters and controlled the interests of five world champions, including Rocky Marciano and Max Baer. As teenagers, the duo had been sworn enemies; Madden had been the leader of the infamous Gophers, while De Mange had been a top enforcer with the rival Hudson Dusters gang. Together, they formed one of the most enduring business partnerships in the history of New York crime.

A lovable rogue, Big Frenchy was admired and respected by fellow gangsters and cops alike. Known for his bristling wit and broad humanitarian outlook, he was the Huggy Bear of gangland. He carried an air of benevolent authority wherever he went. He had a well-lived-in face, with folds of flesh protruding from under his chin like tired, pink putty. His hair was heavily gelled and parted into unruly tufts. Though he had an arrest record for homicide, burglary and safe-breaking, Big Frenchy had never been convicted of any crime.

On the afternoon of 15 June 1931, Coll contacted De Mange and suggested a meeting several hours later. He said that he wanted to cut a deal with the Duke. Though a phone call from Coll should always have been treated with caution, in his zeal to avoid any possible rift Big Frenchy threw caution to the wind and agreed to meet him at Broadway and Fiftieth Street.

This mid-Manhattan location was obviously designed to ward off any possible skulduggery on the part of Coll. Crazy as he was, there was no way that Coll would stage a heist on Broadway in the middle of the day.

The sun was throbbing in the sky as the appointed hour approached. People welled at street corners to find some relief from the sweltering summer heat. Yet Vincent, ominously enough, was wearing an overcoat. Big Frenchy's sedan pulled up at the curb. He left his bodyguards at the car as his lumbering frame strode purposefully towards Coll with a wholesome smile and an outstretched hand. The young Gaoth Dobhair man pumped his hand, but through his buckaroo grin he issued a chilling command.

'Walk,' he ordered, in a low, measured tone.

De Mange felt the bulge of a muzzle wrinkling his undershirt. He was stunned at the audacity of the act – in broad daylight in one of the busiest streets in New York City. It took a while for the extreme gravity and urgency of the situation to register. Coll's icy countenance suggested, however, that this was not the time to dilly-dally.

'Why, man, this is silly,' Big Frenchy was reported to have protested. 'If it's money you want you can have it. But don't try this gun stuff.'

'I ain't here to argue,' Coll retorted, in a tone of sullen irritation. 'Get inna car.'

'OK, Vince,' Big Frenchy was reported to have said, 'but lemme tell those two mugs who are supposed to be body-guards what I think of 'em!'

When Coll told him that he could do so later, Big Frenchy felt slightly comforted by the indication that there might in fact be a later. As the car wound its bone-bruising way through the scenic route up Riverside Drive to West-chester County, the situation moved from the macabre to the saccharine. With the countryside flashing by at an insane rate, Coll and De Mange supposedly shortened their journey with a man-to-man discussion on how much they reckoned the latter would be worth in the current market!

Madden's legendarily calm countenance was jolted when he received a phone call at his Forty-seventh Street office. He instantly recognised the familiar reedy, piping voice of Vincent Coll at the other end of the line. The call was as short as an ass's gallop, but the message was crystal-clear – Coll was to receive $100,000 by midnight. Failure to comply with this demand would result in Big Frenchy being fitted with a cement overcoat. A threat from Mad Dog was not to be taken lightly.

Bold as brass, Mad Dog ambled into Madden's headquarters at midnight precisely. The atmosphere was tense. The room was flanked wall to wall by the Duke's henchmen, who had their hands buried deep in their pockets and were fingering their pieces nervously, in anticipation of trouble. Madden's face was ashen and for once betrayed emotion. His blue eyes clearly showed that he was irate. He sat in stony silence, as motionless as a sphinx, as Mad Dog delivered his chilling message.

Coll indicated that he was not heeled and that if by any chance he had not returned within the hour, Big Frenchy would be killed.

Madden threw a sealed envelope on the desk. According to a file in the Manhattan District Attorney's Office, the envelope contained $37,500. That was all that he could muster at such short notice, Madden explained. He had liquidated a lot of assets all afternoon, raising $20,000. The surplus had come from his own emaciated private kitbag. Coll told him to empty his wallet. He had $800 – mere drinking money in such exalted circles. Grabbing the loot, Coll warned him that his plea of poverty would make him the laughing stock of the underworld. He didn't hang around, though, to gauge the impact of his words.

Two hours later, Big Frenchy was returned safely to the Club Argonaut, with feel-good hugs all round. True to the underworld code of *omerta,* he refused to reveal any details of the kidnapping. As for the police, according to the *New York Times* 'they busied themselves with elaborate denials that any crime had been committed.'

Once again, however, Coll's victory had been illusory. Daggers had been drawn and it was evident that Owney would not rest easy until he had avenged this act of subordination and humiliation. Coll was following a tortuous path, and time would tell if he would be mortally impaled on the spike of his ambition.

*

Having got away with one gangland kidnapping, Coll fancied his chances of success with similar exploits. He had found his *métier* and a handy means of financing his high-rolling lifestyle as his income shrivelled. Next up was Billy Warren, a man who functioned as a banker for bookies and gamblers alike, as well as being one of the best-known punters of his era. He operated on a cash-and-carry basis and was often called upon to honour large sight-drafts presented by turf accountants who had been caught short when long shots had come in. This meant that Warren was like a two-legged ATM, carrying up to $200,000 in person. He carried especially large sums of money when he was at a race meeting.

On one of his sorties upstate, Coll decided to pay Warren a visit during the Saratoga meeting. The meeting had been carefully chosen to combine the maximum potential return with the minimum possible risk. With the aid of a bribe, Coll had arranged that a place would be reserved for his Buick sedan next to Warren's parking space. The sky was grey and grainy as Coll and Fats McCarthy entered the paddock and kept Warren under close observation while Frank Giordano stayed in the car. At the end of the fourth race, Warren returned to his car, where he was confronted by his two tails. He recognised Coll instantly, and, as his adversary's reputation went before him, was in no mood to argue. He parted with $83,000 in all. Although Coll's timing had been a little suspect, as it had apparently been a very slow day at the meeting, it was nevertheless one of the biggest heists in kidnapping history. In short, it had been a well-planned and well-executed operation.

Though Warren remained tight-lipped, the news of the snatch had filtered through to organised-crime circles. One man who was not amused by Coll's scoop was Owney Madden. It was becoming increasingly evident to Madden that the Donegal gangster would have to be tamed if a similar incident, possibly involving Madden himself, was to be avoided in the future. Coll's wildcat antics were threatening the equilibrium of his empire and he would have to be taken out sooner rather than later.

*

Though Coll was certainly one of the greatest exponents of gangland kidnappings, he was by no means alone. Prior to the Lindbergh baby kidnapping of 1932, kidnapping had not been considered a federal offence. The previous year, while Coll was at the height of his powers, an estimated 2,000 criminals were plying this particular trade. The Purple Gang of Detroit, for example, specialised in kidnapping bootlegging rivals and extracting ransoms from them.

Due to the obvious difficulties that might arise with the Internal Revenue Bureau, few victims ever notified the authorities about their kidnappings. Thus, although Coll was almost certainly one of the most successful kidnappers of all time, it is impossible to determine the exact amount of his ill-gotten gains and how many people fell victim to his ransom demands.

He is credited, for example, with the kidnapping of Broadway impresario Rudy Vallee, who had a smash hit in the sixties with 'How to Succeed in Business Without Really Trying'. Popular legend has it that Vallee was forced to part with $100,000 after Coll had burnt the soles of his feet to a crisp. Others claimed that the parsimonious crooner managed to beat his rabid captor down to a mere $10,000 before securing his release.

Vallee, however, always dismissed these accounts as mere urban legends. He told veteran journalist Paul Sann, author of *Kill the Dutchman,* that there was not a scintilla of truth in the tale:

> Larry Fay (another gangster) used to come into the club, the Villa Vallee. He took a liking to me and sometimes gave me a lift downtown in his armoured car. One of my friends spotted me in the car with Larry one day and nearly fainted at the thought that I was being taken for a ride. That's how the kidnapping thing got around but I can't imagine how Coll got mixed up in it.

One man who did feel the wrath of Coll, however, was Sherman Billingsly, owner of the legendary speakeasy, the Stork Club, on West Fifty-eighth Street, described by gossip columnist Walter Winchell as 'New York's New Yorkiest place'. Billingsly's success at the club had been hard-earned.

He had struggled to make a fist of it when he first moved to the city from Oklahoma. With prosperity, however, came the hassles of extortion. Dutch Schultz, Bo Weinberg and Julie Martin all tried to cut themselves in as equal partners. 'I laughed,' Billingsly later recalled, 'and they countered with a guarantee of union troubles.'

Vincent Coll was not so easily brushed aside, however. He kidnapped Billingsly and held him for three days in a Bronx garage, beating him to a pulp, until he eventually exacted a ransom of $25,000 from him.

*

The early years of the 1930s saw New York's traditional gang leaders, known as Moustache Petes, locked in mortal combat with an emerging group of shrewder businessman-gangsters with a criminal vision. Vincent Coll was caught somewhere in the middle. As a non-Sicilian he could hardly be categorised as the former, yet he lacked the latter's business acumen, which was needed to survive the evolving landscape of the gangsters' world.

Extortion and blackmail were Coll's calling cards. While some gangsters believed in using force only when necessary, Vincent used it almost indiscriminately. The newer breed shied away from publicity and saw the necessity of changing with the times. Priorities shifted and problems were redefined. These gangsters preached criminal cooperation not just on a metropolitan level but nationwide.

Charlie 'Lucky' Luciano, Meyer Lansky, Bugsy Siegel, Joe Adonis, Frank Costello and others secretly formed the Seven Group, to buy and distribute illegal liquor to all the participants in the group. Within a year more than twenty-two gangs had been signed up along the Eastern Seaboard. This marked the birth of an organisation that would exercise considerable power and became known as the Syndicate. In May 1929, the future of the mob had been carefully planned in a three-day convention in the President's Hotel in Atlantic City. Representatives from twenty-five cities were present, though the Moustache Petes were notable by their absence. One by one, the most formidable names in American crime filed into the hotel, on the pretence that they were honouring holiday invitations issued to them by Big Frenchy De Mange. To avoid turf battles and maximise their profits, the major crime families in New York, Chicago and Buffalo agreed to divide up the rackets between them. A National Crime Commission, with a board of directors, was formed. According to the commission's rules, nothing was agreed until everything was agreed. Nobody could be 'taken out' without a majority decision, and cops, journalists and members of the public were to be immune from attack.

Realising that Prohibition would not last forever, the Syndicate believed that it was time for the mob to grow up and become a 'legitimate' American enterprise. The activities of the gangs in the various cities would have to be co-ordinated if the rash of bad publicity stemming from Chicago-style gang wars was to be avoided. The seeds of organised crime had taken root in what was a precursor of the modern-day Mafia. Solidly based on cooperation and modelled on the principles of corporate America, the Syndicate prospered in the decade that followed. Gangsters killed each other far less often than before and consequently raked in much more money.

The godfather of the Syndicate was Charlie 'Lucky' Luciano. An equal-opportunities mob boss, Lucky is generally credited with being the man who organised organised crime. He was Coll's polar opposite, being emotionally reticent and noted for his economy of phrase and gesture. He was born Salvatore Lucania on 24 November 1897 in the poor Sicilian village of Lercara Friddi. His family emigrated to America in 1907, settling in the largely Jewish neighbourhood on Manhattan's Lower East Side.

By his early teens he had dropped out of school and attained a considerable criminal record of mostly petty theft. He used his first job, as a delivery boy for a hatmaker, as a means of peddling drugs – he hid his loot in the hat boxes. At the age of eighteen he was sentenced to a year in prison for possession of heroin, and his embarrassed parents refused to visit him there. On his emergence from prison he joined the Five Points Gang, which specialised in harassing voters on election days to vote for the corrupt Democratic machine of Tammany Hall.

Having being raised in a Jewish neighbourhood, Charlie Luciano had the unique distinction of being the first mob leader to cross ethnic lines and work with gangsters of any origin or background. Indeed it is often said that Luciano trusted his Jewish colleagues more than his fellow Sicilians. As a teenager he befriended the handsome but temperamentally fickle Bugsy Siegel and his intellectual sidekick, Meyer Lansky. Their guru was Arnold Rothstein, the man reputed to have fixed the 1919 World Series. He hired the young threesome, and under his tutelage, through a combination of prostitution, bootlegging, gambling and drugs-racketeering, they became millionaires before they had reached their thirtieth birthdays. Luciano claimed that every precinct in New York was under his control. On a given day, once a month, he would deliver $20,000 in used notes to Police Commissioner Grover Whalen. He even increased this sum to $35,000 after the Wall Street Crash to cover Whalen's margins.

Luciano rose in the ranks until he became the right-hand man of Joe 'the Boss' Masseria, a Moustache Pete who still relied heavily on the ancient dark art of Black Hand extortion. Between 1930 and 1931 Joe the Boss was embroiled in a bloody turf battle with Salvatore Maranzano, with both men vying for the position of *Capo di Tutti Capi* – 'the Boss of all Bosses'. This power struggle, which claimed dozens of lives, became known as the Castellammarese war. Maranzano tried to convince Luciano to switch allegiance to him, but when Luciano refused he was taken on a one-way ride. He earned the distinction of being one of the few who survived such a ride, however. On a cold winter's morning Charlie Luciano was kidnapped at gunpoint by Maranzano's goons as he inspected a load of heroin at the Hudson River Docks. He was beaten to a pulp and stabbed with a sharp knife and an ice pick. He was left for dead at Huguenot Beach on Staten Island but, remarkably, survived. The attack left Luciano with a droopy eyelid, a nasty facial scar and a nickname.

Having survived this brush with death, Lucky was determined to resolve the pointless bloodletting of the two ageing Sicilians – on his terms. The *ancien régime* had not shifted with the times and held views diametrically opposed to his own. The Castellammarese war had generated the kind of publicity that the burgeoning crime syndicate could

Vincent 'Mad Dog' Coll.

Vincent Coll's birthplace in Gaoth Dobhair, County Donegal.

The school at Cnoc a' Stollaire, County Donegal,
where the eldest Coll children went to school.

The New York State Reformatory at Elmira, 1913.
(The Chemung County Historical Society)

Dutch Schultz: Coll's childhood adversary.

Living it up during Prohibition: Arthur Palumbo, Peter Coll,
Lottie Kriesberger and Vincent Coll on a Coney Island set.

Vincent 'Mad Dog' Coll.

Owney Madden: the Duke of the West Side.

Lucky Luciano: a gangster-businessman.

do without. On 15 April 1931 Luciano took his *don,* Joe the Boss, out to lunch in a fashionable Coney Island establishment. At one point, Luciano excused himself and went to the men's room. Coincidentally, it was at this point that four gunmen, including Bugsy Siegel, entered the restaurant and shot Joe the Boss, who fell face down in his spaghetti Bolognese.

After Masseria's death, Maranzano went to inordinate lengths to embrace Luciano and appointed him as his right-hand man. Though time had helped to cauterise his wounds, it could not obliterate the memory of how they had come about. Luciano had no time for his new boss or the latter's old-world traditions. He believed Maranzano was past his sell-by date, but he would bide his time until a suitable opportunity arose to offload him.

This fact had not escaped Maranzano, who realised that Lucky would have to be killed as a precaution. The task could not be entrusted to an Italian, however; it is a measure of the esteem and fear in which the Irishman was held that the old *don* plumped for Vincent Coll. As underworld accolades go, this was indeed an honour for Coll: he had been chosen by Maranzano, the boss of all bosses and quintessential Sicilian, who had coined the phrase *'la cosa nostra'* ('this thing of ours'). The baby-faced assassin did not come cheaply, though. He demanded – and received – $25,000 up front, with the same amount due on completion of his duties. The plan was that Maranzano would invite Luciano and his fellow Italian Vito Genovese over to his office for a business discussion, where they would be ambushed by Coll.

On 9 September 1931, Maranzano rang Luciano. Maranzano told him that he had not seen him for days and had pressing matters to discuss with him and Genevose. Could they possibly call around at two o'clock the following afternoon for a conference? But the best-laid plans often go awry.

Luciano had been waiting for this call for several days, having received a tip-off from his colleague Frank Costello about Maranzano's real intentions. On the appointed day, Lucky sent a hit squad of four men, dressed as federal agents, over to Maranzano's office near Grand Central Station. The hit squad was an all-Jewish line-up that included Bo Weinberg, the headstrong Bugsy Siegel, and Sam Levine, an Orthodox Jew who refused to kill on the Sabbath. Maranzano, accompanied by five bodyguards and his secretary, was in his office waiting for Coll when the agents arrived. Maranzano, who had been advised by his lawyers to cooperate with all police officers, identified himself to them. The bodyguards were lined up against the wall and disarmed, while Maranzano was stabbed repeatedly in the chest and body and pumped full of lead. The killers dashed out of the office and down the stairs, followed soon after by Maranzano's bodyguards, who had no wish to pursue them but were afraid to be found in the office with their boss's dead body. Sam Levine later revealed that on their way down the stairs they were met by the unsuspecting Vincent Coll.

'Beat it, Vince,' Bugsy Siegel advised, by way of professional courtesy, 'the cops are on their way.'

Coll was happy to oblige. He was, after all, chortling all the way to the bank. Having pocketed a down payment of $25,000, he now had no task to complete nor anyone to whom to refund the advance. Nice work, if you can get it!

7

THE DOGS IN THE STREET

While Coll had spent the early part of 1931 trying to re-landscape the hierarchy of the New York underworld, it had not escaped his notice that his rivalry with his former employer had not yet reached a satisfactory outcome. Neither man had wavered in his intentions, however. As temperatures soared in one of the city's hottest recorded summers, Coll's war of attrition with Schultz escalated to unprecedented levels of bloodletting.

Vincent's lunge for underworld supremacy had so far been characterised by reckless, madcap exploits, the details of which did not appear to have been fully worked through. It seemed that no task was too onerous for him to undertake. Allied to this, he seems to have genuinely believed that he and his clutch of acolytes could realistically take on the high priests of crime – Oweny Madden, Dutch Schultz, the Artichoke King, Lucky Luciano and so on – and emerge victorious.

There was no denying, though, that Coll's harum-scarum approach and tactless impetuosity could only lead to tragedy. He lived for the moment, seeking instant gratification, and lacked the foresight or mapped-out vision of a smoother brand of villian, like Luciano, Lansky or Madden. Compared to his underworld rivals, Coll lacked polish and was operating on a very primitive level. Remarkably, however, he had somehow escaped the gaze of the public at large thus far and, compared to most of his rivals, was still regarded as relatively small beer in New York's hall of infamy.

This was all to change drastically on a balmy evening in July, in an event that not only earned him his sobriquet but marked his greatest defiance of law and order. In one fell swoop, he was propelled to notoriety as the most-riviled man in the union and public enemy number one. The reign of terror that he had inflicted on New York over the previous few months paled into insignificance when compared with the events of that evening.

At 6.30 pm on 28 July 1931, a dust-green sedan with five occupants careened through the hustle and bustle of East 107th Street, between Second and Third Avenues in Spanish Harlem. Scores of children, freckling in the gritty sunshine, were playing on the sidewalks and keeping an eye on their younger siblings. The street was at basting temperature as the heatwave that had already claimed the lives of seventy-five people moved into its third day. This area was a predominantly Italian ghetto – a fact to which the shopfront signs for *macelleria, pasticceria* and *drogheria* bore testimony. The neighbourhood was described by the journalist George W. Johnston as being 'as populous a block as there is in all New York'. There was certainly no sense of impending catastrophe. Moments before the the terror unspooled, the sound of the laughter of children at play in front of a spouting fire hydrant had caused adults to congregate on the doorsteps of the khaki tenemants to watch the fun. In the midst of the throng, seeking relief from the heat, was Joey Rao, a man who had locked horns with Coll a couple of months previously. He was the proprieter of the nearby Helmar Social Club, a hang-out for slot-machine and peanut-machine racketeers that was soon to close down in a rash of bad publicity.

The car wheezed to a halt as its occupants unleashed a savage fusillade of sixty bullets on the unsuspecting residents. Rao, the intended target, who three times before had proved he had a charmed life in the face of gangster bullets, dived into a doorway and escaped without a scratch as the car bore down upon him and the small, blackened muzzles of the shotguns and .45-calibre revolvers peeked over its side. Instantly there was a sharp crackling like the explosions of a string of firecrackers. Men and women flattened themselves on the pavement or rushed indoors, but the panic-stricken children ran in circles in the line of fire. A lemonade stand, where fourteen-year-old Frank Scalesi was plying a small trade at a penny a drink, was shot to pieces, although the boy himself escaped injury. The hail of bullets shattered windows, splintered brickwork and lodged in the interior walls of the slum dwellings from 208 to 21 East 107th Street. Shards of glass shingled the street and the acrid smell of cordite stained the evening air.

When the dust had settled and the sedan turned north on Seventh Avenue without any display of unusual speed, five children lay seriously wounded on the sidewalks. One of the small, bewildered victims of the mindless mayhem, Michael Vengelli, aged five, was pronounced dead in Beth David Hospital a few hours later. The son of Italian immigrants, John Vengelli and Catherine Carbo, little

Michael was the innocent victim of the dizzy spiral of hate that had claimed over a dozen lives in four months.

Immediately after the incident the boy was rushed to hospital, where his parents maintained a bedside vigil, but blood transfusions and the best efforts of surgeons over a six-hour period failed to save the boy's life. He passed away at 3 am the following morning. His death certificate states that the cause of death was 'bullet wound of right buttock. Great sacro-static notch and large intestine: shock.' His hapless mother, Catherine, wailed hysterically and declared the family to be virtually penniless. 'I can't even buy a black dress!' she shrieked.

Physicians held out little hope of survival either for Michael's seven-year-old brother Salvatore, who had taken to his heels during the carnage until his left leg was shattered by a bullet. At the hospital he was found to be wounded in the left arm and left side of the neck as well. Also expected to die was three-year-old Michael Bevilacqua, who was struck twice in the back as he sat in his pram. Remarkably, both survived, as did two other children who had been less seriously injured. Also hit was twelve-year-old Florence D'Amello; a bullet had pierced her right shoulder as she ran to pick up her cousin, little Michael Bevelacqua. Another survivor, five-year-old Samuel Devino, was shot in the right leg.

New York was appalled by the numbing amorality of the shooting spree. The city had suffered a seismic shock that would send ripple effects throughout the entire country. The unthinkable had happened. This wanton display of hatred had stirred the conscience of the nation and the media were clamouring for justice. 'Harlem Gang Gunners Mow Down

5 Children,' roared the *Daily News,* while the *Daily Mirror* led with 'Gang Rats Shoot Five Children in Beer War's Worst Outrage'. Such was the wave of revulsion against the killings that the *Mirror* speculated that the carnage would prove to be a watershed in the struggle against those who waged war on society. The gangsters had effectively written their own death notices, the newspaper asserted. The paper carried all the sordid details of the shootings. On the front page, three shocking pictures showed Michael Vengelli's innocent, swarthy young face, the tiny frame of Michael Bevilaqua with a drip suspended from it and Sam Devino praying for his dead friend. Accompanying the photographs was a front-page editorial entitled 'A Message to the Baby-Killers':

Here, take a look at these pictures. It represents your latest achievement. You don't recognise the children? But you didn't have time to stop and look at them, did you? You just moved down East 107th Street slowly. Slowly, so that you could use more bullets. And five-year-old Michael Vengelli stopped some with his little body. He fought hard to live, this baby, but he died. But he'll find heaven, a place you'll never see. And if Michael Bevilaqua, two-and-a half, dies of the wounds in his back, it will mean more blood on your dirty hands. Here, you rats! Frame this! It is your masterpiece!

Politicians throughout the country were united in their outrage. 'When they start shooting down babies, it's time to call a halt,' declared Mayor Jimmy Walker as he directed the police to 'drive those dirty dogs out of the community.' In a precursor to Mayor Giuliani's policy of 'zero tolerance', Walker allocated a policeman for every square mile of the city to prevent any possible repetition of the barbaric scene.

Governor Roosevelt, a future US president, was apoplectic with rage. 'The most damnably outrageous thing in a long time,' he commented. 'I can express righteous indignation, but that won't help catch the gangsters.'

The New York Police Department offered a $10,000 reward from the funds of the Patrolmen's Benevolent Association for information that might lead to the arrest of the perpetrators of the crime. In addition, several newspapers offered sums totaling $20,000 for anyone who would furnish information that would bring the gunmen to justice, dead or alive. On top of this, officers of the American Legion, backed by thousands of members, offered to form committees of vigilantes to wage armed war on the underworld. State Commander Edward J. Neary announced that he was willing to turn over the resources of the Legion in the fight against lawlessness and moral pollution, as epitomised by the senseless killing of young Vengelli.

Predictably enough, one of the most stinging reactions to the killings came from the New York Society for the Prevention of Cruelty to Children, which placed its full staff of special officers at the service of the authorities. It also proposed that the Gold Medal for the Outstanding Act of Child Protection be awarded to Florence D'Amello.

The public was baying for blood and the city's dailies were in no doubt about who to point the finger at. There was never any question that Vincent Coll would be assumed innocent until proven guilty. He was traduced and publicly

104

immolated by a rabid press intent on extracting their pound of flesh. 'The Mad Mick' was now dubbed 'Mad Dog Coll', the baby-killer who had brought gang warfare to unforeseen and uncharted depths of depravity. Coll was reported to be the head 'of the most ruthless mobs of killer rats that were ever spawned in the gutters of crime'.

It was open season on the Gaoth Dobhair man, as the headline-writers used words like 'plug-uglies' and 'human vermin' to describe his gang. It was pure outrage to order. The members of Coll's death squad, it was reported, had been full to the gills on gin and Coke when they laid down the stream of fire from their 'bulletproof tank with unbreakable glass'. Perhaps the most damningly insulting accusation that was levelled against the cowardly mob was the fact that they had gloried at the sight of blood and had derived some perverse kind of excitement from the shooting. On seeing the detritus of their shoddy workmanship, it was alleged that one member of their ranks had shouted callously, 'Don't give them a second thought – just cheap brats – to hell with 'em.'

Such was the groundswell of abhorrence in the city that Police Commissioner Edward P. Mulrooney – always a canny reader of the public mood – was prompted to issue a shoot-to-kill directive against Coll and his 'yellow ilk'. 'Draw first and give it to 'em,' he instructed. Addressing 1,000 patrolmen in the Broadway Theatre, the commissioner, whose weather-beaten countenance seldom registered emotion, was visibly unhinged by both the tragedy itself and the affront it represented to the law and its enforcers. 'If you meet the men who committed the outrage in Harlem, give it to 'em above the waist. If I meet them, I'll do it myself,' he proclaimed. The day after Mulrooney issued this shoot-to-kill edict, the police gunned down four suspects – three of them black – who had absolutely no connection with Coll.

Fifty Italian-speaking detectives were dispatched to Little Italy in the hope that they might unearth fragments of information that would provide the investigation with a lead. Though the victims of the fatal fusillade were all Italian, the code of *omerta* still proved watertight. Amazingly, virtually everyone had denied seeing anything. Not even the word that the Vengelli boy had died and that a substantial reward was on offer served to unlock the lips of the hundreds of local residents, who were fearful of gang reprisals.

Twelve-year-old Joseph Corcella, however, cast aside this fear and gave the police their only definite statement. He claimed to have run after the car and gave the police a fair description of its occupants as well as its number plate. Corcella's morsel of intelligence notwithstanding, the 300 occupants of the crowded block between Second and Third Avenues remained tight-lipped.

'It's a Sicilian block,' a frustrated Commissioner Mulrooney conceded. 'They all heard but none of them saw. Or so they say.'

The police immediately sought Rao to help them with their enquiries and in order to eliminate him from their investigation. A thorough search of the Helmar Social Club revealed no liquor. To this day it is unclear whether the attempt on his life was part of the continuous feud between Coll and Schultz or whether it marked a separate, private battle for control of the East Harlem narcotics and policy rackets. Rao was Schultz's top mobman but was also a formidable figure in his own right. He had publicly boasted that he was 'Harlem's Beer King' and had defied Coll to unseat him. Vince had evidently accepted the challenge. Never prone to understatement, the *Daily Mirror* reported Coll as hating Rao as much as the devil hates holy water.

Just before he was fired upon, Rao had been seen talking to two of his associates outside the club. The two 'heelers' had left him a few minutes before the murder car came along and by so doing had probably saved their own lives. Rao had long been regarded as Harlem's 'muscle-in' man, and his relationship with Schultz had been far from harmonious. Rao had quit Schultz's ranks the previous year to join forces with the Arthichoke King, Ciro Terranova, arch-enemy of Al Capone and head of New York's *Unione Sicilione*. He then proceeded to arouse the enmity of his former employer by underselling the Bronx mob in Manhattan. Rao was something of an underworld clay pigeon and had survived three previous attempts on his life. Like Legs Diamond, he was believed to be 'lead-proof' and had commissioned a specially constructed Pierce Arrow, known as 'Battleship Steel', for his protection. The first assassination attempt on him occurred less than twenty-four hours after he had deserted Schultz. Some time later he was shot at as he made his way down 125th Street and Lexington Avenue. On that occasion, once again, the would-be assassins disdainfully disregarded the welfare of children at play: they killed a ten-year-old girl, Jennie La France. He was shot at again in May, when Coll's followers bumped off two of his top men – Frank Amato and Dominic Bologna. It was at this juncture that Rao was believed to have realigned himself with Schultz, as it was in both their interests to eradicate the Mick.

In view of previous assassination attempts, historian

Richard O'Connor suggests that Rao used a human shield as protection:

> Knowing he was marked for slaughter, Rao was said to have kept a pocketful of pennies for distribution to the children on the block around his headquarters, the Helmar Social Club in East 107th Street, so that he was always surrounded by swarming children, and Coll's gunmen couldn't open fire on him.

Rao, however, was too close to the greased palm of Tammany Hall boss Jimmy Hines to get drawn into the baby-killing. Hines later rewarded Rao for his silence. While serving a term in the House of Correction on Welfare Island for heroin- and cocaine-pushing, he was allowed effectively to run the institution and presided over kangaroo courts, knowing that Hines would take care of any screws who dared to poke their noses where they were not wanted.

As the greatest man-hunt in the city's history was mounted, Coll himself was reported to be openly strolling the streets. On the night of 9 August, *New York Evening Post* staff journalist Patrick Frank reported sitting opposite Vince in a downtown West Side interborough train. He reported that the gangster was wearing a 'gay silk shirt' and a blue suit, whose bulges indicated that he was armed. He was accompanied by a slight man with sharp, ferrety features – probably Giordano. After unostentatiously checking the identification of his fellow passenger by comparison with a newspaper composite sketch, Frank and his wife followed the two at a discreet distance when they alighted at Chambers Street. The two mobsters strolled nonchalantly through City Hall Park and turned north on a route that took them to within a few blocks of Police Headquarters. It was at this stage that the two men quickened their pace, and Frank consequently lost sight of them. The police combed the area, but to no avail.

Rumours were rife as to Coll's whereabouts, and there were dozens of reported sightings of him. Following up the leads proved to be an exercise in futility, however. 'Coll is a common type,' Captain James Sweeney stated. 'Anyone is likely to think that he has seen Coll. There are hundreds of persons right here in Manhattan that bear a striking resemblance to him.'

Anything to do with the man made good copy. The *Daily Mirror* reported that he had slipped the police cordon and that his gang planned a showdown with rival mobsters in Saratoga. They would pass as racing enthusiasts until the time came 'to mount guns':

> In Saratoga was fought one of the important battles of the Revolutionary War. It was known by the attacks of Iroquois Indians and the French. But, boasts gangdom, when their battle starts bullets will ricochet in the streets as never before and perhaps some more children will be killed.

One day, the police received a tip-off that Coll was to board a five o'clock train for Saratoga out of Grand Central Terminal. Commissioner Mulrooney dispatched three score of his most able officers, but the gangsters had apparently got wind of the ambush and once again evaded the police net.

At one stage the New York City police believed they had

Coll cornered in a downtown section of the city, but again he seemed to have given them the slip, for he was later reported sighted in Albany. On another occasion, he was spotted in a drugstore, but detectives, who arrived within minutes of the sighting, were unable to find the man that looked like him.

Thus Coll managed to escape the dragnet, probably without having to leave town at all. He dyed his sandy locks black, grew a moustache and purchased a boater and a pair of tortoiseshell glasses, which gave him the appearance of a foppish freshman. All things considered, it has to be said that Coll's gentrified disguise ill became him.

He needed an alibi, and it may well have been around this time that he approached his cousin from Gaoth Dobhair, Biddy Coll or Biddy Eoghan Charlie. Biddy lived in Brooklyn with her husband and had known Vincent and Lottie quite well. According to the story told to a relative of Coll, Assemblywoman Bríd Rodgers, when she was young, Vincent and his mob paid Biddy an unexpected visit one night. He threw his holster up on the table and begged her to say that he had been eating supper with her on a certain night. Fearing the wrath of Vincent's infamous temper, Biddy's husband showed signs of relenting, but she would have none of it. She chased him out of her house, letting him know in no uncertain terms that she wanted no part in his illicit activities.

Though the police were cocksure of whom they were after and had dusted the murder car for fingerprints, so far they had little to go on. Facing a rising wave of public indignation, they strained every muscle to make a break-through.

The first important advance in the case came with the arrest of Tony Trabino, a twenty-one-year-old dope addict and pusher who had found East 107th Street to be a particularly profitable hunting ground. Trabino had been a felow inmate of Coll's in Elmira and had been his colleague in Schultz's operation, before the Mick decided to plough his own furrow. On the evening of the 'Baby Massacre', Trabino had been reading a paper in a car parked adjacent to the Helmar Club. Once the news of Trabino's detention was leaked, Coll knew he was in trouble. There was no love lost between the two, and Trabino was unlikely to protect him. Even if he managed to withstand the rigours of Mulrooney's infamous 'sweatbox', he was bound to sing like a canary as soon as the cops denied him his habit.

Trabino claimed to have been the intended target of the shooting. He also professed to having dragged a little girl to safety during the bloodbath. Described as 'slight, well-dressed and keen-looking', Trabino was arrested on the evening of 5 August 1931 and subjected to eight hours of unremitting interrogation. During this period the door leading into the room was kept closed as detectives worked in relays, firing a drumbeat of questions at him as their stenographer broke endurance records filing his replies. Trabino inevitably wilted in this sweatbox.

Having secured their underworld informant, Commissioner Mulrooney immediately moved to have Trabino committed as a material witness. His attorney, David Goldstein, accused the police of using heavy-handed tactics to obtain a confession while his client was in their custody. Two broken ribs and a mass of bruises provided graphic illustration of their brutality. The police statement had clearly been gained under duress. In a charged exchange that provided a brief glimpse of the Zeitgeist, Goldstein concluded his attack on the police by remarking that 'after all, we still have a government of law'.

'A government of racketeers,' interrupted Assistant District Attorney Pilatski, as the courtroom erupted into a babble of protests. Attorneys, magistrates, detectives and Trabino's mother and sister all took part in the ensuing Donnybrook, which was a sad reflection of the breakdown of the legal process. Trabino's sister struck one of the detectives and as the turmoil abated Trabino was remanded to the House of Detention, where he was to be held as a material witness. It was clear, however, that another eyewitness would have to be found. Though listed third on the charge sheet, Trabino incidently was never called upon to testify against his gangland adversary.

It is unlikely that Coll saw the humour of Trabino's courtroom fracas. He was holed up at the time in a shabby, two-storey residence at 1815 Randall Avenue in the Clasons Point section of the East Bronx. He knew that he could ill-afford any mistakes. Even if the cops did not have enough evidence to pin the baby massacre on him, he nevertheless faced a long stretch up-river. On 3 March 1930, a pair of Bronx detectives had found two pistols under a car against which Coll happened to be standing, in Manfredi's Garage at 161st Street and Grant Avenue, the Bronx. The police asserted that Coll had thrown them there when he saw them enter. He was charged with the illegal possession of firearms and was released on $10,000 bail – no mean sum for the thirties. He had been convicted on a similar charge in 1924 at the age of fifteen, and in New York a second violation of the Sullivan Law was automatically classified as a felony rather than a misdemeanour. After many deferrals, his trial date was eventually set for Bronx County Court on 11 July 1931. His former employer, Dutch Schultz, had posted the bail bonds back when they had been pals. Predictably enough, Coll failed to show up and Judge Barrett directed forfeiture of his $10,000 bail. By jumping bail Vince had hit the miserly Dutchman where it hurt most.

It is hard not to reflect on what would have happened if Coll had appeared for his trial. Would he have grown old, fat and disillusioned in prison as Lottie moved on to pastures new? And what of Michael Vengelli? Would he at present be a hale and hearty septuagenarian living on a pension in one of the city's boroughs and regaling his grandchildren with tales of pre-Giuliani New York, where gangsters roamed the streets with impunity?

8

DOG-LEGS

All roads led inexorably north. Coll had for some time been exploring the possibilities of muscling into the upstate fiefdom of Jack 'Legs' Diamond. In his mind the logistics were simple. He and Diamond would rebuild the whole upstate set-up and carve up the spoils between them. Legs had fallen on hard times and was in seriously reduced circumstances by the time Coll made his approach. After the initial success of his criminal empire, his career had gone into freefall as the roaring twenties petered to a whimper. Like many young achievers, he had gone into an early decline and was in the throes of a protracted legal wrangle. Financial need had forced him to offload many of his interests. This, of course, enhanced Coll's bargaining power.

Along with his loyal stooge, Gary Scaccio, Legs faced a kidnap-and-torture rap for snatching a couple of hick bootleggers to convince them of the benefits of handing their entire enterprise over to Diamond. Grover Parks and James Duncan finally agreed to his demands after intensive and sustained torture in an Albany hotel, where they were burnt with cigarettes, had lit matches placed under their fingernails and had their backs branded with red-hot pokers. Both men eventually grassed to the police and Diamond and Scaccio faced trial for their kidnap and torture. Legs also had a federal income-tax rap to contend with and was steeped in debt.

Despite these setbacks Diamond still wielded considerable power in upstate New York, and his well-oiled organisation remained largely intact. Coll figured that they could set up an *entente cordiale* of sorts and relocate their operation to the territory north of Albany. There were many all-season tourist resorts in the Adirondacks – Lake George, Lake Placid, Saratoga – where booze was at a premium. Their base would also serve as a platform to smuggle merchandise across the Canadian border. Diamond would take care of that end of things while Vince managed New York City. Gauranteed a constant flow of liquor at competitive rates, they would wipe out the Syndicate. The spoils of the booze, slot-machine, dope, nightclub, speakeasy, bail-bonds, waterfront, dry-cleaning, taxi and window-washing scams would be divided equally between them. Their illegal empire would then look to wipe out the likes of Madden, Terranova, Higgins, Luciano, Costello and Schultz. This scheme would never be more than a business arrangement, however, and when underworld supremacy had been achieved, Coll would explore the possibilties of dissolving the partnership. Though his idea would require an initial leap of faith, Vincent envisioned an easy and seamless transition. In his innocence, he probably even looked to the day when he would broaden his horizons and diversify his outfit to other cities like Chicago, Los Angeles, Kansas City, Philadelphia and Boston.

Coll's skewed vision was doomed from the outset,

however. The partnership would never grow to a significant size: it was a desperate attempt by two has-beens to maintain their ascendency in the underworld.

*

Although Coll and Legs appear on the face of it to have been strange bedfellows, they were in essence two of a kind. They were both of Ulster stock and had had brothers shot by their implacable enemy Dutch Schultz. Both lived in a world of diminishing returns, in which they tried to achieve everything in their youth, and neither man looked likely to see middle age. In life-assurance parlance, both men would have been considered high-risk liabilities.

Diamond himself was a colourful character and the first mobster to have achieved celebrity status. He toured Europe and had a permanent slot in gossip columns. When he was eventually shot down in a dingy Albany flophouse – after four unsuccessful attempts on his life – his wife and paramour competed with one another on the vaudeville circuit with separate kiss-and-tell shows about life with the mobster.

Diamond was a pendulous man with a cheesy complexion. He had a well-chiselled jaw framed by dark, moody eyes. By constantly boasting that 'the bullet hasn't been made that can kill me', he inevitably put a hex on himself. He and his criminal cohorts blazed a trail of destruction through the Jazz Age yet were accorded the distinction usually reserved for the luminaries of showbiz. He managed to turn infamy into celebrity. His criminal exploits are forever immortalised in Pulitzer Prize-winning Albany author William Kennedy's rollicking yarn *Legs* and in Warner Bros' classic 1960 film

The Rise and Fall of Legs Diamond. Kennedy's mythologising, which at times veers close to hagiography, provides colourful accounts of a womanising, likeable rogue, as charming as he was audacious. For his part Kennedy denied suggestions that he had gone soft on the gangster: 'I'm not out to preach morality . . . gangsters are human beings and this was the scene usually left out of the movies.'

Jack Diamond's sexual prowess was considerable and he surrounded himself with a bevy of beauties. His first wife, Florence Williams, could not stomach his womanising, bootlegging lifestyle and constantly threatened to report his illegal activities to the police. Diamond promised her a date with the fishes in the East River if she ever seriously entertained such an idea. Unsurprisingly the marriage did not survive more than a couple of months. Diamond's next wife was Alice Kenny, a plump, dowdy secretary from Long Island whom Jack married in 1926. She remained housebound during their five-year marriage. Alice worshipped her husband, to the extent that she had the words 'my hero' inscribed on a picture of him that hung above the mantelpiece. After his death, she convinced the public that she had been oblivious to her husband's illegal practices until his death. She was not as innocent as she appeared, however, and may even have had a hand in her husband's murder. In reality, Alice was an ignorant, intolerant and insecure woman who gambled, drank and suffered from eating disorders. Diamond's biographer, Gary Levine, describes her as 'a crass, nagging, beer-guzzling ignoramus who could curse like a mule driver'.

She competed for Legs's affection with the flame-haired Marion Strasmick, a showgirl from Boston who was better known as Kiki Roberts. Kiki was quite an eyeful, with high cheekbones, pert lips, a sharply patrician nose and milk-white skin. Working as a Ziegfeld Follies showgirl had kept her figure in excellent shape, but it did not do much for her foul mouth. Legs lavished jewels and furs upon her, decorated her apartment and opened a private bank account under her name. Kiki was a woman of expensive tastes. Jack was a big spender, though, and his ill-gotten gains were laid at her disposal.

Alice was aware of her rival but constantly pointed to the ring on her finger. 'She may have some of my husband's attentions,' she would boast, 'but I have the man.' William Kennedy's bizarre accounts of Alice and Kiki staying at times under the one roof at Acra appear to have been based on fact. On such occasions both women carried pistols and exchanged threats, while the house staff feared a bloodbath. 'I'll pull that little red-haired bitch apart if she doesn't get out of here,' Alice threatened. This prompted Legs to have Kiki housed in an inn at Tannersville, several miles from Saugerties, where a third girlfriend was based.

There are many theories as to how Diamond attained his moniker. Some suggest that it referred to his reputed prowess on the dance floor, while others insisted that the name stemmed from his ability to flee from the scene of a crime. He was also fairly adroit at running out on his friends. Frail and tubercular, Legs was the son of John and Sara Diamond, who had met at a dance in Cavan. The constricted horizons of poverty-stricken rural Ireland forced them to emigrate to America in 1897. A baby boy, Jack, was born to them soon after their arrival in the squalid Philadelphia neighbourhood of Kensington. Neither he nor his brother Eddie lived up to

Sara's expectations in the field of education, and Sara's health began to fail so drastically that she had to consume large quantities of heroin and morphine to make her life worth living. Like the dysfunctional childhoods that had resulted in the criminal natures of Coll and Schultz, once again the father was the villain of the piece. John Diamond spent most of his time conforming to the Irish-emigrant stereotype of a drunken bowzy, while his two sons accumulated a formidable corpus of felonies to their name. After Sara's death in 1913, John Sr took them to Brooklyn, where they joined up with the Hudson Dusters gang, who stole packages from delivery trucks in Manhattan. During the war years, Legs was in and out of the New York City Reformatory, and in 1918 he was drafted to serve with the US Army in the First World War. Once again his legs carried him from danger and he promptly went AWOL. After eventually being apprehended by the military police, he was sentenced to five years in Leavenworth Prison for desertion. He served only a year and a day of this sentence, however.

On his discharge, Legs went to work briefly as a bodyguard for the all-powerful Arnold Rothstein before taking up a position with one of Rothstein's partners, 'Little' Augie Orgen. Under Orgen's tutelage, Legs rose through the ranks, becoming one of his most trusted lieutenants. Also in Little Augie's gang were 'Lucky' Luciano, Louis 'Lepke' Buchalter and 'Waxey' Gordon. It was a formidable line-up: Diamond and Gordon handled the distribution of Little Augie's illegal liquor, while Luciano took care of the prostitution and drug rackets and Lepke controlled the garment district and its unions. This gang's main rival was Kid 'Dropper' Kaplan, who had a virtual monopoly on the

Manhattan bootlegging trade. Diamond set up a dim-witted stooge to assassinate the Kid as he was being led away to custody in a police car. As a reward for having arranged the killing, Legs received a significant slice of Kaplan's bootleg and narcotics rackets.

Diamond amassed enormous wealth and flaunted it lavishly. He was ostentatious, driving flash cars and surrounding himself with a harem of gorgeous molls. He used his famous Broadway speakeasy, the Hotsy Totsy Club, as a means of servicing his insatiable libido. The club developed into a Mecca for the glitterati of the Prohibition era, and its regular customers were a who's who of gangdom.

The first internal problem in Little Augie's empire came in October 1927, when Lepke had the gang boss shot at point-blank range as he left his headquarters at Norfolk and Delancey Streets. Legs was caught in the crossfire, receiving bullet wounds to the leg and arm. Police found him swimming in a sea of blood and rushed him to hospital, where he fell into a coma. When he regained consciousness he growled the underworld code of *omerta* at the policemen who had maintained a vigil at his bedside.

Little Augie's elimination provided Legs with an opportunity to annexe the dead boss's bootlegging empire. Others, most notably Dutch Schultz, had the same idea, however, and a two-year war of attrition ensued. Diamond initially held the upper hand as his team controlled all the major highways upstate along which the bootleg whiskey was ferried from the Canadian border. He also had the backing of the rackets king, Arnold Rothstein, until Rothstein was assassinated in 1928.

Early in 1929 Legs was acquitted for the murder of two

petty hoodlums in the Hotsy Totsy Club due to lack of evidence. More than two dozen people witnessed the murders, in the Dan McGrew style, but fear of reprisals kept them from singing. During his trial, there had been no let-up in hostilities with Schultz. The Dutchman's partner, Joey Noe, arranged a meeting of the two factions in the Harding Hotel with the aim of establishing some form of settlement. Schultz handed Legs a suitcase containing $500,000 in return for Legs relinquishing the midtown beer territory. Legs had a reputation for double-crossing, however, and as Schultz and Noe left the hotel contented with the newly brokered peace, two men ran from an alley and shot Noe dead.

The Dutchman's blood was up, and, as was the case with Coll, he figured that if he could not get at the man himself, the next best thing would be his brother. Eddie Diamond had suffered from a variety of lung ailments for some time. Legs had paid for his rehabilitation in the kinder climate of Denver, where the Dutchman's goons sprayed his car with more than a hundred bullets. Astonishingly, Eddie survived; he died later of TB in a New York sanatorium. Eddie was the only person, including his various women, towards whom Legs felt any loyalty, and so he vowed to avenge the shooting. Nine of Schultz's best guns met their deaths in the blood-letting that ensued. On an October evening in 1929 the Dutchman's hit squad eventually caught up with Legs in Kiki's suite in New York's Hotel Monticello. They came across the couple dining in their pyjamas and laid down a stream of fire that ripped the room asunder. Kiki emerged unscathed but Diamond was shot five times. Needless to say, he survived the attack and took time out to recuperate in Europe. His trip made front-page copy throughout the continent. His reputation went before him, however, and some countries refused him entry. On his way over, Scotland Yard tipped off James Fitzgerald-Kenny, the Irish Minister for Justice, that Legs was aboard a ship called the *Baltic*, and the Yard requested him to detain the gangster for questioning in a stock swindle. The alarm faded, though, when the captain of the *Baltic* wired back the news that Diamond was not in fact on board.

Legs eventually arrived in Plymouth on another ship. A large crowd of curious onlookers gathered, hoping to catch a glimpse of the famous gangster, but the authorities refused him entry. He played to the gallery, however, beaming at the paparazzi and appearing on most front pages. The Belgian customs officials took a similar view of him and accompanied him on a train ride to Aix-la-Chapelle, where he was handed over to the German authorities. Several days later, they forced him to board a ship bound for his native Philadelphia.

On his return to America, Legs re-established himself in Acra, upstate New York. In the morning of 27 April 1931, a car containing a number of gunmen disguised in hunters' outfits pulled up outside the Aratoga Inn. Legs, who was having a few drinks with Kiki and some friends, was awaiting an important phone call from his attorney. As he paced the floor nervously, the sharp report of gunfire shattered the quiet in the building. Once again an attempt had been made on his life, and once again he survived. Eighty-one bullets in total had been fired; two of them had found their intended target. Legs was rushed to Albany Hospital in the Cairo town hearse; a bar towel did little to stem the flow of blood from his body. His personal physician, Dr Thomas M. Holmes, who had more than earned his keep, arrived on the scene, and although the bleeding was halted Legs suffered massive and continuous haemorrhaging. After three days at death's door, he once more confounded medical science by surviving. During a three-hour operation, most of the bullets were dislodged. Although one remained in his lung, once the infection had subsided Legs was taken off the critical list. During a four-week recuperation, a classic photograph appeared in the daily newspapers showing a doe-like Diamond, his sutured body barely visible, staring innocently at his wife as a set of rosary beads dangled over the side of his bed. There was nothing innocent in his defiant vow of retribution, however. 'Well I made it again, nobody can kill Legs Diamond,' he crowed. 'I am going to settle a few scores just as soon as I get my strength back, you just wait and see.' Dutch Schultz was reported to be incensed at the fact that Legs had survived, and he fumed in exasperation, 'Can't anybody shoot that guy so he won't bounce back up?'

Despite his upbeat show of recalcitrance, the constant perforation of his wiry body was bound to be taking its toll on Legs. Behind the sassy sound bites, Legs's strength – and his determination – were ebbing. By the time Coll entered his sphere of influence he was already on the highway to oblivion. He had been hit by fourteen bullets in four attempts on his life. It was only a matter of time before the bullet would be made that could kill him – or that the jury would be formed that he could not rig.

*

Fleeing upstate was not a step to be taken lightly by Coll, particularly in light of an incident that had taken place there a number of days before the baby-killing. On the morning of 19 July 1931, twenty-four state troopers, accompanied by half a dozen NYPD detectives and several area police chiefs and deputy sheriffs, raided George White's farm at Freehold, a mile north of Cairo. Leading this crack team was Johnny Broderick, the famous metropolitan detective, who in a rare moment of expansiveness described Vincent Coll and Fats McCarthy as 'the two toughest guys I ever met'.

The team were acting on information that Coll had sent a task force up there to eliminate Legs and annexe his operation. This may not have been a million miles from the truth, as Coll had sent his six best guns to Cairo – Arthur Palumbo, Mike Basile, John di Rosa, Louis Bifano, Frank Facchiano and John Burnett. No contact had been made with Diamond, so we must assume that the six were saying more than their prayers, as White's Farm was only four miles west of Diamond's headquarters at Acra. On top of this, Vince's sister, Florence, her husband, Joe Reddan, and his brother-in-law, Bill King, had been dispatched to Coxsackie, ten miles upriver from Cairo.

It was around 4.30 am when the crack force of police pulled up quietly to White's Farm with their lights doused. The building was a large house shrouded in darkness. As the raiding party crept towards the house in the freckled light, they noticed that the front door was ajar and that the hall was unlit. They began to think that they were acting on bogus information until one of the raiders noticed a thin wedge of light under a door to the right. Trooper Harry Fritz, six foot two and with hands like shovels, kicked down the door and flung himself on Arthur Palumbo, who had pulled a gun from under his pillow. Fritz kicked the .45-calibre revolver out of Palumbo's hand and delivered an uppercut to his opponent's jaw. The rest of the troopers had fanned out to the other rooms, and eight men and six women were apprehended. All were captured without struggle, except for Mike Basile, who drew a shotgun and felt the full weight of Broderick's southpaw for his troubles.

In addition to snagging all these gangsters under the one roof, the cops unearthed a small arsenal, which Lieutenant Francis McGarvey referred to as the biggest haul he had ever witnessed during a long and distinguished career with the state police. The cache included two machine-guns, five rifles, three Tommy-guns, seven sawn-off shotguns, five .45-calibre automatics, five .38-calibre 'killer type' revolvers and several thousand rounds of ammunition. One trooper speculated on the carnage that might have ensued had the Collsters not been taken by surprise. 'The Coll gang is one of the toughest gangs in the nation. They would sooner shoot first and ask questions later,' he told the *Cairo Herald*. This message was hammered home to the police several hours later when, in a garage in Cairo, they came upon a blood-stained Buick which had obviously been used to take somebody for a ride.

The fifteen prisoners were hauled off to the Greene County Jail, while the police concentrated their efforts on the august magnificence of 10 Washington Avenue, Cox-sackie. Once again the building's three occupants were caught unawares as the troopers stumbled upon another cache of two machine-guns, five sawn-off shotguns, a plethora of small arms and a couple of thousand rounds of ammunition.

All in all, it had been a profitable morning's work for the police. Nevertheless, they were disappointed at having missed out on the big prize. They had been acting on information that Coll himself would be at White's Farm on the night in question. As it happens, they were not far wide of the mark, for some weeks previously members of Coll's gang had slipped out of the city, under cover of darkness, with the intention of rendezvousing in Cairo. There they would establish an operational base which would serve as a platform for lightning raids on Diamond's empire from within enemy territory. Vince had been due to travel upstate that very night but had received a tip-off about the imminent raid and had remained in New York. He was unable to warn his comrades, however, as the farm did not have a phone. Other reports suggest Coll had left the farmhouse that day, hours before the swoop.

*

Fleeing to Greene County in the wake of the White's Farm botch-up was a calculated risk. The flurry of police activity in the area had clearly revealed Coll's hand. Moreover, none of Diamond's goons were likely to have had any moral objections to carrying out Police Commissioner Mulrooney's shoot-to-kill fatwa. Coll had to live long enough to convince Legs that his mission was one of coalescence rather than elimination. Under the circumstances, returning to the scene of the crime did not seem like the brightest idea in the world, particularly as the police had narrowly missed capturing him several weeks previously. Was Coll stupid enough to return to the very place where the nucleus of his gang had been apprehended? Or would he in effect manage to outwit the police again by going to the very place where they would least expect him to hide? Could the unthinkable – that Coll had had an attack of common sense – have happened?

There was also the small matter of trying to locate Legs. A month earlier, he and his bodyguard, Gary Scaccio, had stood trial for the kidnapping and torture of Grover Parks and James Duncan, the two applejack pedlars who had been given the once-over in an Albany hotel. Counsel for Diamond, Daniel Prior, had secured a change of venue – from Catskill to Troy – for the trial. Such was the ground-swell of opinion against Legs in Catskill that he would not have been given a fair trial, Prior argued. The change of venue was an important concession, for the good denizens of Troy, a sleepy backwoods town in the Hudson Valley, had no intention of raising the ire of gangdom.

With the shadow of mobster reprisals hanging over them, the jury in Troy acquitted Legs on 14 July. The State Attorney General, John B. Bennett Jr, was incensed by the decision. He had earmarked Diamond as the first high-profile scalp in a campaign designed to recapture public confidence. This was regarded as a major setback for the ethical-cleansing lobby. 'It seemed to me that the allies of crime were too strongly entrenched to be defeated, that our times had witnessed the triumph of the antisocial,' was Bennett's appraisal of the verdict. Despite this blow, it was his announced attention to proceed with the prosecution of Legs on a second indictment.

True to form, Diamond had abandoned his co-defendant, the loyal Garry Scaccio, to his own devices. He withdrew his own highly paid lawyers, refused to furnish him with the necessary funds to hire an attorney and declined to testify for him. On 31 July, Scaccio was sent down for fifteen years in Clinton Prison.

Legs, meanwhile, went underground. Even somebody as supremely confident as himself, who had survived several attempts on his life, must have winced when the *New York Times* wrote his underworld obituary:

It seemed to be the prevailing opinion here that Jack Diamond is a past number in Greene County. Whether the advent of the heavily armed Coll mob, a tough outfit with a swollen reputation for homicide in the Bronx, gave him his cue to move on or whether he feared the wrath of the country folk is a matter of conjecture.

On 13 August, Coll was spotted in Albany, the fulcrum of Legs's criminal empire. A rumour circulated in the state capital's sporting circles that a mob of New York gangsters were guests at a mammoth farewell party for Diamond on the eve of his departure for the city's federal court. The underworld rumour was that Coll was seeking the leadership position vacated by Legs, who at that stage looked an odds-on favourite to face a four-year stretch in prison for violation of the Prohibition Law. It was no secret that Coll wanted to reorganise Diamond's bootleg band and start business afresh in the Catskills. What was not widely known, however, was that a greatly weakened Coll, although never much of a team player, sought to work in tandem with Legs rather than eliminate him.

Reported sightings of Coll in Albany were evidently not without foundation. Accompanied by the roguish Tuffy Odierno, Lottie had travelled upstate some weeks previously to secure a hideout. Some time around late August or early September Vince and Lottie, posing as husband and wife, moved into a Spartan apartment at 325 Hamilton Avenue, Albany. It was a ground-floor flat – ideal for a quick getaway. Using the assumed names of Mr and Mrs Howard Corbett, they signed a fourteen-month lease on apartment 1A at the cost of $90 a month, paying three months' rent in advance.

Coll's main contact in upstate New York was the diminutive Jimmie De Lucia. The previous May, Coll had posted him to Waterlivet, a strategic outpost halfway between Canada and New York. De Lucia had had to make himself scarce in New York after the murder of Roy Sloane, who had been mistakenly identified as Coll in the Mad Dot Boat Club, a speakeasy he jointly owned with his sister. He now ran a soda-fountain stationery shop at 1508 First Avenue, Waterlivet, and was a font of underworld intelligence. Coll contacted Jimmie on his arrival in Albany, and though the latter was unwilling to reveal where Legs was hiding out, he promised to tap his pipeline. For his part, Vince offered to meet Diamond on the latter's home turf in order to allay suspicions of another assassination attempt. He would be willing to meet him, unaccompanied and unheeled, at Young's speakeasy at 513 Broadway, Albany, Diamond's favourite lair. For two days Vince remained bolted up in his apartment, under self-imposed house arrest, while he awaited news from Legs. On the morning of the third day, Vince and Lottie were awakened by the ringing of their doorbell and the roar of a car racing down the street. Gun in hand, Coll went to the door, under which a typed note had been shoved. According to Victor Rosen, this note would have read something like this:

Tonight 11. Back room Youngs. Come alone. NO TOOLS!

Vince arrived late, to maximise the gamesmanship. He was frisked on arrival and was escorted to a private room at the back of the bar. Diamond, who was fond of a tipple, sat on a couch drinking black coffee. This night, of all nights, was one on which he had to remain sober. A sheen of sweat glazed his forehead as he stared stonily at the young pretender. The atmosphere was fraught with menace as five of Legs's henchmen held Coll in a steady gaze, ready to pounce at the slightest hint of aggression. The two protagonists exchanged a lingering glance. Vincent, an accomplished negotiator, was unfazed by the presence of his adversary's henchmen and struck a hard bargain. He reminded Diamond of his current lowly status in the underworld hierarchy and of the fact that the two men shared many common enemies, most notably the Syndicate and the Dutchman. By pooling their resources, Vincent could provide Legs with a chance to salvage some dignity and rebuild his empire. Coll proposed that, instead of battling with each other, the two should form some kind of symbiotic association that would control the bootleg trade over the Canadian border and virtually cut off the supply to their rivals' business in the city. Diamond would run the upstate operation – smuggling the booze and setting up a 2,500-gallon still; Coll would handle distribution in New York and engage in hostilities with the Syndicate and Madden until he and Legs had established a monoply on distribution.

Legs baulked at the suggestion of a fifty-fifty split. He had for some time relied on Joe 'One-Eye' Rock to distribute his liquor; Rock was unlikely to be too enamoured of cutting the man who had maimed and blinded him into their operation. Eventually they agreed upon a forty-thirty-thirty split, with Coll getting the lion's share of the takings and Legs and Rock the remainder. It was incumbent upon Coll, as well as taking a healthy gang into the organisation, to raise the initial capital for the venture and the cash that would be needed to keep Legs out of prison. He would of course expect a healthy return for his outlay. And so a deal had been brokered that would see both through their current difficulties.

So how was Coll to come by the neccessary cash? Old habits die hard, especially those that go unpunished. Since his successful abduction of De Mange, Mad Dog had turned a profitable fund-raising device into an obsessive tick. His kidnapping exploits had so far paid handsome dividends, though the risks were high. He had already lined up a candidate for his next foray into gangland kidnapping.

Connie Immerman ran an extremely lucrative nightclub in the heart of Harlem. Connie's Inn specialised in jazz and black music, which were becoming increasingly trendy amongst the doyens of Greenwich Village. Connie was known to be a walking cash register but was virtually untouchable because of his standing with both the guardians and the violators of law and order. Coll was never one to be unduly deferential to substantial reputations, though; once again he would opt for the direct approach. As with De Mange, he planned to stage the kidnapping at a time when the club would be at its busiest.

On Saturday 9 August, shortly after midnight, Coll and four of his accomplices entered Connie's Inn. Tuffy Odierno, Pasquale del Greco and Fats McCarthy went straight to the toilets, coming out separately and lingering by the entrance. The place was jointed, and nobody suspected that anything was afoot. Coll surveyed the scene until he found what he was looking for – or rather he thought he had found what he was looking for. George Immerman, Connie's brother, stood at a ringside table with a man and a woman. Coll shoved the muzzle of his gun, draped with a napkin, into George's back and gestured towards the door. Whether it was a genuine case of mistaken identity or whether Coll, on realising his mistake, decided to cut his losses and go for a lesser amount of loot, we will never know.

Coll's companions chaperoned George to the door, where he was bundled into the car that Frank Giordano had stationed, with its engine running, in front of the inn. The car then sped up Seventh Avenue and zigzagged back and forth in the warren of narrow streets that made up the Bronx, until George had no idea where he was. They pulled up in front of a threadbare apartment, one of a string of identical blocks. Coll fixed drinks while George was body-searched. Vince demanded $25,000 but the search revealed that Immerman was carrying a mere $12,123.79. Coll took twelve grand, leaving his captive the remainder for his taxi fare. Mad Dog then made Immerman write a note to Connie, instructing him to hand over $13,000 in cash to the bearer. Odierno and Giordano went back to the club, while Coll and Immerman reportedly killed time playing poker. A couple of hours later, the boys arrived with the unmarked cash and Giordano dropped George at 145th Street and Seventh Avenue, where he boarded a cab bound for Connie's Inn. On his arrival there, George was dismayed to find that his absence had been reported to the police and that it had been officially recorded as a 'disappearance'. He phoned the precinct and went to great lengths to explain that he had only been visiting his uncle, at two o'clock in the morning. 'He keeps late hours,' was his explanation, as the entry was erased from the memorandum.

It had been a lucrative night's work for Coll, who had netted a neat twenty-five grand in a couple of hours. He must have wondered, though, what price he could have exacted from the well-heeled Connie himself had he been more accurate in his identification. The booty was not his to keep, however, and on the night of Sunday 9 August he handed his takings to Diamond in a Chinatown speakeasy as the first instalment of their agreement. More significantly, the cash was essentially an imprimatur on their newly established partnership.

Legs feared the worst. His attorney had warned him to expect Judge Frederick Hopkins to hand him a long sentence and a hefty fine for violating the federal Prohibition law. The testimony against him was overwhelming and the jury returned a guilty verdict. Judge Hopkins sentenced him to four years at the Atlanta Penitentiary and fined him $11,000. Prior announced that he wished to appeal the verdict and Legs was released on $15,000 bail. The word on the street, however, had it that the underworld would tidy up whatever loose ends had eluded the state prosecutors.

9

DOGGIE BAGGED

The search for Coll soon developed into the biggest manhunt in the history of the state. It also saw the largest number of men ever assigned to a single case. The investigation, which had initially been based in New York and the neighbouring states, had extended to places as far apart as California, Colorado and Florida and had even spilled across the Canadian and Mexican borders. So far, however, it had produced few results. Vincent, meanwhile, was holed up less than a block away from police headquarters in Albany.

The *Daily News* reported Coll to have acquired the savoir faire of a 'big shot' and to be revelling in the limelight:

> Coll, in the brief fling at gangland fame he enjoyed, became even bolder as his prestige grew. Being sought as a nationally known criminal was, to the tough kid from the Bronx, the equivalent of four-sheet billing to a small-time actor – he loved it.

He used his hideout in Albany as a pied-à-terre, travelling to and from New York on a weekly basis. While his trips were hazardous, they were a risk Coll had to take. Though he did not want to attract undue attention, he realised that he had to keep a grip on his organisation in the city for fear of either dissension amongst his ranks or the possibility that his opponents would recapture his hard-won spoils.

That said, he was determined to set up a bridgehead in Albany much like the one he had hoped to set up in Cairo. His sister, Florence, rented a cottage for him in the picturesque village of Averill Park, ten miles east of Albany. It had an idyllic sylvan setting, flanked by hills and facing Crystal Lake.

His relationship with Legs, meanwhile, was coalescing nicely. Coll clearly knew how to humour him. They had begun to make their mark in the Adirondack resort regions of Lake George and Saratoga. By mid-September, three months before Legs was killed, they had lined up a dozen speakeasies between Albany and Plattsburg and had installed two drops for storing liquor smuggled in from Canada. Plans were also afoot for an airstrip near Malone, six miles from the border. This would enable them to fly the booze in during the night.

In the meantime, as summer faded into fall, frustration was beginning to get the better of Police Commissioner Mulrooney. The clamour for justice had not abated and the public was beginning to despair at the NYPD's lack of success. Mulrooney decided to smoke Coll out. A series of lightning raids on the speakeasies that Coll controlled saw seven of them close in the space of a fortnight. His wise-guys were continually harassed – they were picked up, charged with number of trumped-up crimes and released on bail.

Coll's misfortune was the Syndicate's opportunity. They

figured they should hammer home their advantage during his mid-career lull. They destroyed the speakeasies, beer-drops and trucks that he controlled, hijacked his booze and began to retake some of the territory he had seized several months previously.

The Dutchman, meanwhile, was winning the propaganda war, boasting that the Mick was all washed up and no longer in control of his assets. He had no comeback from the avalanche of events which had overrun his life in the past few weeks, Schultz claimed.

If Coll had some tricks up his sleeve, they had thus far remained very well hidden. He was on the horns of a dilemma. He realised that he would have to prove to the underworld that he still wielded some influence in the city and that his operation was intact. He also realised, however, that he would reassert his prestige only if he pulled off an audacious, eye-catching act that would make his rivals sit up and take notice. Though Lottie counselled caution, Vince bore forward with singular purpose.

*

On 2 October 1931, Joe Mullins stood chatting to Whitey Connors in a garage on 151st Street near the upper reaches of Park Avenue. This was no ordinary garage, however, but a drop for the empty beer barrels from Dutch Schultz's empire. Mullins was the foreman of the drop and its chief checker. It was business as usual, and the subject of the Mad Dog was probably touched upon as both men went about their daily duties. The day was hot and muggy. New York was experiencing something of an Indian summer and fat wedges of sunlight fanned out across the garage. As the two men lit their cigarettes, they heard the squeak of brakes. Someone shouted from the street, 'Who's Joe Mullins?'

Mullins handed his assistant a sheaf of papers and strolled unsuspectingly towards the door, exhaling tusks of smoke from his nose. Suddenly a shot rang out, and Mullins stumbled sideways before collapsing in a dishevelled heap. The assassin stalked his target, firing twice more with cool precision. As he did so, the tweed cap he was wearing fell off his head, but he did not bother to pick it up. By the time Connors had reached the front door, Mullins lay unconscious in a pool of blood, as the fresh smell of cordite scented the air. He was rushed to the Morrisania Hospital, where he died on the operating table at 3.09 pm. An autopsy revealed that Mullins had died from gunshot wounds to the head which had fractured the skull and penetrated the brain. One bullet had found its mark directly in the middle of his forehead, while another had struck slightly above the left eye. The assassin's aim had been true. Two fragments of a .38-calibre bullet were taken from his head and a similar intact bullet was found lodged in the muscles of his neck.

Within minutes, word of the shooting reached the Bronx homicide squad, under the command of Deputy Chief Inspector Henry Bruckman. The police investigation made an immediate and significant breakthrough, in the form of two New York Edison Company workers who had been splicing wires in a manhole on 152nd Street at the time of the incident. Minutes earlier, Michael Gill and his assistant, Terry Carroll, had pushed their necks through the manhole to shout obscenities at an eldery woman and a youth who were engaged in a bit of a fracas at the kosher market on the corner of the street. The woman wielded a broom while the youth insisted that it was not his turn to sweep up. As the commotion petered out, Gill saw a cream-coloured Buick slow to a halt outside the garage and a short, squat man with black, tousled hair get out of the car and stand in the doorway.

'Then I heard two shots and I saw a man stumble out of the garage and fall on his face,' Gill confided. 'There was a gleam of steel in the other man's hand. He walked away, but all of a sudden he tripped. It didn't seem to worry him, for he picked himself up calmly, brushed his trousers and climbed into the car.'

He yelled at Carroll to write down the number of the murder car – 9Y 97-59. Detective Louis Brancato was immediately dispatched to trace it.

'By that time I was on the sidewalk and the car was heading for me. It was driving too slowly for my comfort. I ducked behind the tool cart when it passed me,' said Gill.

He proceeded to give the police a detailed description of the assassins: 'The gunman was hatless, his shirt was open at the neck. He had on dark trousers. The other man had on a soft hat, with the brim snapped down. He was a dark-complexioned fellow.'

Once again the media showed its disgust at another wanton murder in the war of attrition between Coll and his former employer. By targeting Mullins – a $35-a-week route man – Coll had sunk to even lower depths of human degradation. Coll had sent a message to the Dutchman, it was argued, that even the lowliest of hirelings were now considered legitimate targets. It was also suggested that Mad Dog intended to kill Schultz's wife.

But the newspapers had got it wrong once again. Mullins was no mere hireling but a vital cog in the Dutchman's machinery. This was not a random killing: it was a token of intent, designed to strike at the very heart of Schultz's operation. Mullins may not have been the Dutchman's brains but he was certainly his memory. Coll knew that Mullins was a walking ledger with a photographic memory and was entrusted with the knowledge of the judges, prosecutors, police officers and public officials who were on the Schultz payroll. At a second's notice, Mullins could reel off the amounts paid to these important figures and what services had been rendered in return. He could list inventory and sales figures of barrels and how many were in storage. It would have been perilous to commit such information to paper, and Mullins was assigned to hold it in his head. He had in effect a level of executive importance that belied his paltry income. His role was even more important in light of a police raid on Schultz's headquarters ten days earlier, when virtually all of the Dutchman's records and accounts had been seized. Clearly he was a presence that had to be dealt with.

By taking out Mullins, Coll had ensured that Schultz had lost his memory. The killing would baffle the public but would be symbolically meaningful to the Dutchman. It also constituted a timely reminder to Schultz that Coll was breathing down his neck.

The murder was ill-conceived and poorly executed, however. The car had crawled slowly past the manhole, affording Gill and Carroll a perfect view of the assailants. In the heat of the moment, there was presumably a mix-up between the driver and the gunman and the two men in the manhole were allowed to live to tell the tale. And tell the tale they did! Gill assured the police that he would have absolutely no difficulty in picking out the two gunmen in an identity parade. The police had two eyewitness accounts and the registration number of the Buick to go on. Coll's calculated big hit in the city had backfired and the net was clearly closing on him.

That night a conference was held at the District Attorney's Office. It was attended by William H. Jackson, Assistant District Attorney of Bronx County, who wrote about the events four years later:

> We talked over the evidence that had been gathered during the day. With sparse clues patched together from witnesses' testimony, nothing but circumstances and a hunch pointed to the gang of twenty-three-year-old Vincent Coll.
>
> 'We'll keep a lookout for Coll, of course,' said Bruckman as the conference broke up, 'but you know what that means. He hides himself pretty well.'
>
> It was a grim-faced set of men that left the office that night. Gang guns had flamed after months of silence. It looked as if a long siege was in store.

Brancato's search for the registration plates had run into a brick wall. A week previously, a man called Robert Seligson had transferred a car to one George Stone. Stone's licence plate was 9Y 97-59. On further investigation it was revealed that Seligson had received a car from a George Lynch, whose certificate had been issued on 20 August. Investigations found, however, that all the names and addresses that had been uncovered in connection with the car were fictitious. All that could be gleaned from the probe was that a series of false transactions and transfers had taken place, presumably to hide some sinister purpose.

Meanwhile, eight Prohibition agents seized three truck-loads of beer and ale that belonged to Frank Ahearn and Henry Stevens. Since Noe's death, both men had worked in close conjunction with the Dutchman and had owned the garage where Mullins had been killed. As the officers stood outside the Majestic Garage at 1262 Westchester Avenue, where the haul had been made, a stone crashed through the glass panel of the sliding door in front. As the agents turned apprehensively, the door was blasted open with a terrific detonation under the impact of a home-made bomb reputedly thrown by Vincent Coll himself.

As he emerged from the dog-eared steel door, one of the agents managed to take note of the licence number – 6N 645 – of the car as it wheezed off into the darkness. Within minutes, the teletype system began to clatter out an alert for the car. It was nearly six o'clock in the morning when word came through that a car bearing the licence plate 6N 645 had been located at the Penn Post Garage at West Thirty-first Street. Three detectives – Eddie Byrnes, Joe Gannon and Al Laurino – were promptly dispatched to the garage to stake out the car. Gannon and Byrnes hid on the floor of the car while big Laurino hid behind a pillar. They maintained their positions all day without gaining satisfaction. Shortly before midnight, however, a garishly dressed man who looked like a modern-day bookie swaggered towards the car. Laurino recognised him instantly as the razor-jawed Vincent 'Jimmie' De Lucia, one of Coll's cohorts.

Byrnes and Gannon sprang from their cramped hiding place with guns drawn. Paralysed by surprise, De Lucia stared in disbelief as his hand furtively reached for his side pocket.

'No, you don't,' cried Laurino as he sent De Lucia sprawling to the floor. He gingerly picked himself up and said with an aggrieved air, 'Be more careful about those things.'

'Stop the nonsense,' Byrnes was reported to have countered, according to a contemporary account in *True Detective*. 'Where is Vince and the gang?'

'That's a good one,' answered De Lucia. 'You know we don't work that way. None of us knows where the boss or the others are. When he calls us, we get together for a meet. Otherwise I know as much about it as you do.'

When asked where he had intended to go with the car, De Lucia told them that he had to pick up Tuffy Odierno in Times Square. De Lucia drove the detectives to the supposed rendezvous, where they waited patiently for over an hour. Nobody arrived.

De Lucia was whisked away to the headquarters of the Homicide Squad and subjected to a thorough interrogation. He was weak and would in all likelihood have cracked under the strain of the questioning, but, according to Assistant District Attorney William H. Jackson, the system under which the gang operated had foreseen the capture of one of their number and had an in-built mechanism to forestall betrayal. In hindsight, however, the fact that he was never charged with the bombing and that he immediately uprooted to the West Coast after his release from custody suggests that De Lucia may well have sung. It should be remembered, too, that Jackson's account dates from April 1935 and that he would have been aware of the sensitivity of and inherent danger in pointing a finger at a tout.

During De Lucia's interrogation, the police uncovered a slip of paper in his coat pocket which had a telephone number scrawled on it. Detectives worked well into the wee hours until they finally traced the origin of the message – the Ladonia Hotel.

The three detectives who had been working on the case were joined by three others as they sped towards the East Side. On arrival at the Ladonia they rooted out the manager and showed him photographs of members of the Coll gang. He recognised two of the gang as the occupants of Room 506. Two men were posted in the lobby to cover the elevator and the stairway exits, while the others went upstairs to the room. The manager had given them the key but the door had been bolted fast from within. It fell to the stocky Laurino to hurl his considerable weight at the door. The four detectives stormed the room and within seconds Patsy Del Greco and Mike Basile had been pinned to the ground. No arms were found in the room and the two mobsters were subjected to the ignominy of a strip search. Another significant slip of paper was found in Del Greco's wallet. It was a bill for $20 room rent made out to Messrs Stern and Collins at the Maison Hotel, on the West Side. Two of the detectives hauled Basile and Del Greco to the Bronx for questioning while the other four made their way across town.

The same procedure was followed at the Maison Hotel. Photographs were shown, two men covered the exits, a key was obtained for Room 52, the key failed to work and Laurino's shoulder splintered the door. The long-jawed and debonair Frank Giordano bolted upright as his right hand sneaked under the pillow. A butt of a revolver smashed down on his peeling pate as he was dumped unceremoniously on the floor. A fourth member of the Coll gang had been bagged.

A black leather valise was found in the wardrobe. It was effectively a portable arsenal, containing five loaded revolvers, one of which was equipped with a Maxim silencer.

'Where did you get these?' demanded Byrnes, according to *True Detective*.

Giordano puckered his sloped chin.

'Some man at the Ladonia Hotel. I don't know who he is,' he answered.

'Is that the best story you can give us?'

'Yes.'

'And what is this?' asked Byrnes, pointing to a small metal can.

'That's a can of ether. The same man gave it to me.'

This container was to have far-reaching consequences for Coll's aide-de-camp.

As Giordano was being bundled into the car, Detective Donald Carey whispered to him in a conspiratorial tone, 'Don't be a fool. Look out for your own interests. Never mind the rest of the mob.'

Giordano reflected on this momentarily before agreeing to talk to Detective Brancato. He obviously didn't trust the Irish cops.

'When did you see "Irish" last?' Brancato asked in Italian.

'Last night in the Cornish Arms.'

'Who else was there?'

'Tuffy Odierno, Fats McCarthy, Patsy Del Greco, Mike Basile and Eddie Bruno.'

'Bruno? I never heard of him being in your mob.'

'Oh, he's one of the boys we picked up during the summer when we were upstate. He gave me two hundred dollars last night and told me to take care of the guns for him.'

Brancato changed the subject as he clapped a companionable hand on the suspect's shoulder.

'How is it, Frank, that you haven't got an auto,' he asked, in a friendly, confidential tone. 'Some of the other boys have such swell cars.'

Giordano knew what Brancato was angling at. A virtuoso liar, he enjoyed sparring with the police and wasting their valuable time. He felt confident that he could evade their clutches. Bit by bit, he cobbled together a story which he thought would be credible.

'I bought a little car about six weeks ago,' he teased.

'What kind?'

'An Essex 1926 coach for twenty-two dollars.'

'That's no car for a fellow like you,' said Brancato. 'What did you do with it?'

'Oh, I just took the bill of sale for it. I never even drove it away. As a matter of fact I bought it for Bruno.'

The team of detectives decided to split up. Brancato and two new arrivals would interrogate Giordano further while the others would raid the Cornish Arms Hotel.

Giordano revelled in the attention he was receiving and led the detectives across Queensboro Bridge to Long Island City, where he said he had purchased the car. While making this journey, he told the police in great detail about his role in the gang and the duties he had to perform. He was essentially the driver and quartermaster of the gang – Coll's aide-de-camp. He was also in charge of arranging hotels for meetings and buying cars.

He was playing a dangerous game of cat and mouse with the police, though, and unfortunately for him he lacked the mental prowess or cunning to outfox them.

He eventually led them to the garage, near Court House Square, where he had purchased the $22 car that he had earlier spoken of. Plump and dusky-skinned, Michael Janicki ambled out of the garage as the police car pulled up.

'Did this man ever buy a car here?' Brancato asked tonelessly, pointing to Giordano, whose angular face and steely stare focused sternly on him.

Janicki quivered with fear before he stammered, 'Oh yes, I know. You are that fellow George Lynch, who only wanted the bill of sale for the car.'

'Lynch, that's a nice name for you,' piped up Brancato, recalling what the Motor Vehicle Bureau files had unearthed.

'Well, I use it sometimes,' admitted Giordano.

'Giordano, for once you are not so smart. I arrest you for the murder of Joseph Mullins.'

*

While all this was happening, a drama of another kind was taking place at the Cornish Arms Hotel, on the West Side. Known to its customers as 'The Corned-Beef Arms', the fifteen-storey hotel still stands today, though it has been totally refurbished as an office block.

At the hotel, the police found their quarry registered under the names of 'Mr and Mrs Moran' and 'Mr and Mrs Stein'. As soon as they were sure of these people's identity, they called Bronx headquarters, and two carloads of men, armed with shotguns, rifles and tear bombs in anticipation of a siege, surrounded the hotel. Four of the raiding party were told to go upstairs and hide in a room adjoining the one where they believed Coll was holed up. Once again the exits were sealed off and reinforcements were sent for. Led by big Al Laurino, the quintet got out of the elevator on the fourth floor and stepped stealthily towards the room. Peeping around the corner, they saw a tall, dark-haired, bespectacled man accompanied by a swarthy, globular man loping lazily along the corridor. Despite their quarry's disguises, the detectives instantly recognised the pair as Mad Dog Coll and Tuffy Odierno, his torpedo man. Vince had changed beyond all recognition. He was no longer the blond trigger-man whose light wavy hair, rotund face and blue eyes had earned him the sobriquet 'baby face'. His hair had been dyed black, as had a newly sprouted moustache, which he had clipped with fetishistic neatness. Horn-rimmed glasses completed his boffiny disguise. But there were still the thick, pike lips and the deep cleft in the chin to distinguish the young Gaoth Dobhair man.

Laurino could not contain himself. 'There he is,' he said in a clearly audible whisper. Coll bolted down the corridor with the cops hard on his heels. Finding himself in a blind end of the hall, he darted into the men's toilet.

The dim-witted Tuffy Odierno was not so quick. He stood glued to the spot, waiting for the inevitable leaden hail, as detectives swooped down upon him. As the handcuffs came out, a look of relief registered on his blanched face. Things could have been worse – it could have been one of the Dutchman's death squads.

'It's all right, Irish,' he was reported to have yelled after his friend. 'It's only the cops.'

Coll stuck his head sheepishly out of the door and surrendered without a struggle. The two stylishly dressed molls who had remained in the suite offered little resistance either. Police recognised them as Lottie Kreisberger and the dark and doleful Betty White, Frank Giordano's girlfriend.

A bankroll was found lying on one of the beds.

'I am going to count this for you now and I want you to watch me,' Byrnes told Coll, as he took the money in his hand. It amounted to $4,600 in hundred-dollar bills.

'You can have the money,' Coll prompted, carelessly. 'I won't need it any more.'

This overt attempt at a bribe fell on deaf ears, however. Two guns and a large quantity of ammunition were also found in the suite.

'We've been looking for you a long time,' remarked one of his captors.

'I know it,' retorted Coll, with a ghost of a smile. 'But if I'd had any information of value I'd have come to you.'

Though the police had now netted eight of the Coll gang, including the big fish himself, their operation had not been flawless. In spite of the ring which the police had thrown around the Cornish Arms, the most calculatingly cold-blooded member of the gang had somehow managed to escape. Fats McCarthy had been reading the papers in Coll's room when he heard the police grab the others. He did not hang around to ask questions. A .38-calibre revolver, wrapped in a towel, that was found on the roof of the hotel was believed to have been discarded by him in his flight to safety. Its previous owner had been one Dutch Schultz and its handle bore five notches, which Fats had hoped to add to before long.

An hour later all the captured gangsters were reunited at

the Bronx homicide squad. A large, jeering crowd had thronged the street outside the station, hoping to catch a glimpse of Mad Dog, who was public enemy number one.

Coll, meanwhile, was in high spirits. Despite the gravity of the situation, he conveyed the impression that he did not give a tuppenny damn about his fate. As he waited to face the barrage of questions, he congratulated the police on his capture.

'It was good work to get me and the rest of the boys without somebody getting drilled,' he told his interrogators. His tone was polite, almost deferential. 'I've been under a heavy strain and I'm sort of glad to get it over. Everything that's happened around here has been blamed on me. As a matter of fact, I've been up in Albany and Cairo most of the time. I just got back Friday.'

Sullen while he was being photographed, Coll suddenly broke into a wheezy chortle as he was led to a cell.

'What's the matter with you?' asked a detective.

'Boy, I'll bet Dutch Schultz will go out and get drunk tonight!' Coll cackled. 'He'll feel safe now with me in the can.'

It is a measure of Coll's moral decay that he could find humour in a situation that would in all likelihood result in his execution.

*

At the headquarters of the Bronx homicide squad, the members of Coll's gang were lined up in an identity parade. Once again, the gravity of the occasion seemed to have escaped him as Vincent set the pace for his henchmen in the presence of the law. He appeared to be in fine form. A photograph taken at the time shows Coll towering above the other members of the rogue's gallery, flashing his lupine smile as his associates follow his lead, grinning defiantly at their captors. Gallows humour indeed!

They lined up under the scrutiny of Michael Gill, the man who had witnessed the slaying of Joe Mullins from his manhole. 'Do you know any men in this crowd?' asked Bruckman.

'Tell this man to take his cap off,' said Gill, pointing to Odierno, who was forced to comply. He then asked Odierno to walk up and down the room quickly.

'That's the gunman,' Gill declared vehemently.

'And the other man, do you see him?' Bruckman prodded.

'That's him,' said Gill, pointing at Giordano.

The mobsters were immediately whisked away to separate rooms. Odierno protested his innocence, saying that he had been out of town on the day of the shooting.

'I was upstate with Lottie and Vince. We didn't get back to New York until 3 October. I can prove it by witnesses,' he remarked smugly.

This was a persistent ploy by gangsters. Many a state's case had been hamstrung by gangsters' alibis.

For his part, Giordano flatly denied any involvement in the incident. Tests conducted by Assistant District Attorney Edward F. Breslin on samples of his handwriting had shown, however, that the signatures of Lynch, Seligson and Stone on the Motor Vehicle Bureau files were identical to that of Giordano.

While Coll was put through the mill for the Harlem baby-killing, Giordano and Odierno were indicted by the

Bronx Grand Jury for the murder of Mullins the previous Friday. They were arraigned before Magistrate Earl A. Smith in Bronx Homicide Court and held without bail.

In light of Giordano and Odierno's indictment for first-degree murder, the District Attorney's Office decided to hold the rest of the gang in custody pending further investigation.

Coll was incensed, as Assistant District Attorney William H. Jackson, who was handling the investigation, learned in no uncertain terms. Coll issued a string of vile oaths at the investigating team. Jackson recalled the incident later:

> One day while I was walking into the visiting room to question one of the men, Coll motioned to me. I went over to speak to him.
>
> 'Jackson,' he said, 'I lose $10,000 every day I'm in the jug.'
>
> That's too bad,' I told him. 'You'll stay until we complete our investigation.'
>
> He turned away, muttering curses.
>
> 'If it's the last thing I do,' he said. 'I will get you for this.'

Basile and Del Greco were held without bail in Morrisania Court, accused of the $3,000 hold-up of a Bronx bakery. This was a new experience for the four Coll men who had been charged. Though they had previously been arrested twenty-four times between them, only one of them – Patsy Del Greco – had ever served time before.

Lottie and Betty White were held in jail, having both failed to raise the $50,000 bail. De Lucia was also held on $50,000 bail as a material witness to the killing of Mullins, but, interestingly enough, the police made no effort to fasten a charge on the man whose arrest a few days earlier had set them on Coll's trail. The underworld took this as an indication that De Lucia had shopped his boss.

But if De Lucia was a gangland quisling, his trim, daring wife, Agnes, was an underworld Paul Revere. Shortly after the round-up had started, with the arrest of her husband, she was in a car racing to Troy in upstate New York, where other members of the Coll retinue were in hiding. Agnes had spotted Jimmie driving the cops out of the Penn station and had hastened to tip off the rest of the gang, who were hiding upstate. Her desperate trip was in vain, though. Captain Richard Oliver, who was attached to the Manhattan police headquarters, had anticipated this move. She unwittingly led the police to Averill Park, where Florence had purchased a hideout for her brother Vincent. Joe Reddan, Coll's brother-in-law, was captured on the spot, along with Agnes De Lucia, as the detectives doused the lights in anticipation of more arrivals. Florence and her thirteen-year-old son Mike, William King – Joe Reddan's stepbrother – and the lithe Frank Facchiano arrived shortly afterwards.

Ordered to stick up their hands, the new arrivals opened fire. Shots whistled through the rooms but the police did not dare to return fire for fear of wounding each other in the darkness. Reddan managed to free himself and for no apparent reason dumped some guns and ammunition into the fire. As the gangsters shot blindly into the darkness, the fire spewed its contents all over the room. Remarkably, despite all the fireworks, nobody was injured. When their ammunition was exhausted, the police threw on the lights. The struggle that ensued was hard but brief, and after a wearisome and bone-crushing ride from Troy, the captured mobsters were reunited with their colleagues in the Bronx. Togged out in plus fours and a Hovis-like tweed cap, thirteen-year-old Mike Reddan, Vincent's nephew, brought his dog with him on the long journey south.

Fats McCarthy's daring escape notwithstanding, it had been an extremely fruitful sixteen hours for the police – the reward for months of slow progress. With their series of dawn swoops, they had apprehended all but one of the most vicious and cold-blooded gang in the Union.

Commissioner Mulrooney was now confident that the whole affair could be brought to a swift and satisfactory conclusion. He spoke to the assembled news hounds about the fruits of the lightning raids, stating that Coll and his crew had returned to town 'to pull something big'. His audience took this to mean in all probability the extermination of Schultz. With Coll and his gang in custody, Mulrooney took off to Philadelphia to watch the World Series.

*

Meanwhile, Coll and Giordano were questioned at length about the Harlem baby-killing by New York County District Attorney Thomas T. C. Crain. Coll clammed up, determined to brazen it out. The police had managed to supply two witnesses for the Mullins murder, but the mobsters were cocksure that the cops would never be able to pin Vengelli's death on them. The wheels of justice moved with unaccustomed rapidity for Coll, however.

Under a veil of secrecy, a dusky-skinned, nervy man who

was to be known as Commissioner Mulrooney's 'private witness' was hastily taken to the Bronx, where the five prisoners, accompanied by four detectives, stood before him in an identity parade. His gaze fixed momentarily on two of them before he stated, 'Them two there – them are the ones what did it!' He was pointing at Vincent Coll and Frank Giordano.

Still under police protection, the witness was whisked back to the obscurity of Manhattan. Only a handful of the top brass at the Police Department and the Prosecutor's Office had known about the witness's existence. It was a mark of the cloak-and-dagger realm in which these men moved that District Attorney C. T. Crain had known nothing about such an eyewitness until barely an hour before he was produced. For more than two months previously, he had been kept under wraps on the direct order of Mulrooney himself.

On the morning of 5 October 1931, Coll and Giordano were charged with Michael Vengelli's murder. A strong police guard was thrown around the block in which the Homicide Court was situated and another in the courtroom on a tip-off that Coll was to be taken out on the spot. In quick succession, the young gang chieftain was arraigned on a short affidavit that charged him with the murder of the child, and he was held without bail and indicted for the same crime by the Manhattan Grand Jury. Magistrate H. Stanley Renaud ordered that he be held without bail and agreed to an adjournment until 15 October on the request of Assistant District Attorney Max Wieder. Wieder stated that, because of the gravity of the crime, the people should be given ample time to prepare their case. The name of the principal witness before the Grand Jury, whom Mulrooney had somehow conjured up, had been withheld for fear of gangland reprisals.

Dressed in a custom-tailored suit and crisp blue shirt, Coll cut a dashing figure in court. He stared blankly at the presiding magistrate as he told him that he was a bricklayer who had been out of work for the past seven months. Beyond that, he was tight-lipped, demanding to talk with the man he wanted as his lawyer, former magistrate Albert H. Vitale. During the hearing, Inspector Sullivan disclosed that Coll had tried to involve one of the women who had been arrested with him.

'This man tried to fasten a gun on one of the women,' the inspector told the court. 'Of all the mobs that have been in here, this collection is the lowest.'

Coll, however, had a retort for all occasions. 'Inspector,' he shot back, in a dry, gravelly voice, 'ain't that just a difference in ethics.'

Coll had been uncharacteristically camera-shy leaving the courthouse, holding his hat in front of his face when press photographers tried to snap him. He had a hangdog look as he glared in frigid indignation at the assembled hacks. For his part, Coll's attorney, Albert H. Vitale, said he had 'no doubt that Coll could prove his innocence'. He told the press that he would be advising the Donegal man to plead not guilty and that he would be seeking a change of venue to ensure a fair trial, in view of the emotiveness of the case.

Then, under an augmented police guard, Coll was taken to Tombs Prison, New York's oldest and dampest gaol, where he conferred with Giordano. 'We'll never go to the chair, kid,' the *Daily News* reported him as saying to his lieutenant. 'They haven't got a thing on us.'

Though the Tombs was not the most comfortable of prisons, Coll seems to have been treated like a celebrity during his stay there. In his autobiography, *The Kid from Hoboken*, one of Coll's fellow remand inmates, Bill Bailey, recalls the day Coll was captured:

One day I was coming up from the visitors' floor. As one guard handed me on to another through the long series of gates, he passed a bit of news to his cohort. 'They just nabbed Mad Dog Coll.' The mere mention of tha gangster's name sent chills up anybody's spine. The police mentioned his name as if he were a saint.

That night we had hot dogs for supper. They were big and round and garlicky. Since I like hot dogs, I complained that two were not enough. But on the floor where Mad Dog Coll was locked up, it was a different story. First there was a banging of tin cups against the steel cell-door bars, the traditional form of prison protest. Then they took the hot dogs and threw them out of the cells. One guard told another, 'There were hot dogs boucing all over the place like ping-pong balls.' Of course, this action brought the warden out immediately. Mad Dog was screaming his head off about the rights of prisoners and the inhumane treatment they were receiving by being served what he himself 'would refuse to serve to pigs'.

The warden, never one to offend a real first-class bottom-of the-barrel hood like Coll, caved in. The whole tier of toughies was served hamburger steaks, which were rushed in to them from several area restaurants. It served the rest of us right – for ten cents' worth of guts, we could have had hamburger steaks that night too. From information I received later, Mad Dog was treated like a dignitary for the length of time he remained at the Tombs.

As the tempo quickened in the preparation of the state's case against Coll, it was learned that the government was proceeding against him as well. It was announced that Coll's income-tax returns – or lack of them – were being probed by special agents of the Internal Revenue Service in cooperation with US Attorney George Z. Medalle. Apparently there was no record of a return having been filed in Coll's name for the years 1928–30.

Police had also identified Coll as one of the pair who had bagged $18,000 from the daring raid on the Sheffield Farms Milk Company a year and a half previously. There was also the small matter of jumping bail after the Sullivan Law rap. Though the cases against Coll developed an almost-irresistible momentum, the police concentrated primarily on the baby-killing. If they could secure a conviction, Coll would surely go to the chair, and his other misdemeanours would be rendered academic.

10

A Dog's Dinner

A crumpled stub of paper found in Vincent Coll's clothing proved costly in his gang's fight for freedom and led to damaging disclosures for his co-accused. The piece of paper had been found when detectives strip-searched the mobster on his arrival at the headquarters of the Bronx homicide squad.

During this process, Coll had requested that a knife in his vest pocket be handed over to him. It was a keepsake that had belonged to his brother, Peter. Detective Eddie Byrnes reached into the watch pocket of the vest, which hung over a chair. As he retrieved the knife, his fingers touched a creased-up slip of paper.

'Sorry,' Byrnes was reported to have said, as he put the knife in his pocket, 'I can't give it to you now, but I'll keep it for you.'

'OK. Thanks a lot,' said Coll.

As soon as he had left the room, the detective unravelled the ball of paper that he had found in the pocket. It was a receipt for a dining-car bill (number C-91838) that amounted to the princely sum of $5.10. Coll had negligently stuffed the stub into his pocket after paying the bill.

In light of the news that Tuffy Odierno was planning to present an alibi which he claimed could be corroborated, Byrnes decided to follow through on the receipt as a new lead. It would be highly ironic if one of the few sentimental gestures in a largely unsentimental life would result in Coll's conviction.

Odierno had claimed to have been on a farm in Claverack, three miles east of Hudson, at the time of the baby-killing. One day, with five female cousins, he had taken a run to Albany, where he had met Coll in a speakeasy. He had kept in contact with Coll after that. After a few months upstate Odierno had decided to travel to the city to see his mother in the Bronx. As Vince and Lottie had wanted to take in some Saturday-night shows, he had boarded a train with the couple the day after Mullins had met his maker.

Sensing a breakthrough, Byrnes went immediately to the passenger agent's office and sifted through a folder that contained the records of the dining-car receipts to find a tally with the number on the slip. Byrnes learned that waiter number three, a tall, black man named Lee R. Boyce, had served a meal to three people in Drawing Room A, Car 370, Train 18, on 1 October 1931. The detective sought out Boyce, who, along with the Pullman porter Henry B. Oliver, identified the diners as Vincent Coll, Lottie Kreisberger and Tuffy Odierno. The significane of this disclosure was that it established the fact that Odierno was definitely in New York at the time of Mullins's murder and, consequently, that his alibi was a tissue of lies.

The origin of the tweed cap that had fallen off the gunman as he stalked Mullins was also revealed. Its label read, 'The Packard Cap, the Classic System Cap'. Having traced the manufacturers, Detectives Bill Mara and Louis Brancato obtained lists of New York stores that stocked the line. Their search led them upstate to Nathan Richman's general store in Catskill. The sales clerk told them that he had sold a similar type of cap to a short, swarthy young man a month earlier. When shown a photograph of Odierno, the clerk admitted that the man in the picture bore a striking resemblance to the purchaser.

The investigators received another break two days later. While out on his beat on the morning of 6 October, a patrolman from the Fifteenth Precinct came upon a brown, 1931 Buick bearing the number 9Y 97-59. Its frame and chassis numbers were checked against a list of stolen autos and were found to tally with those of a car which formerly bore the New Jersey number H 117400. This car had been reported stolen by its owner, Dr Edwin J. Valentine, nine days previously. Dr Valentine came to the Bronx and identified the car as his own; the fact that it featured a makeshift iron bracket for a spotlight made it instantly recognisable to him. The new licence plates had evidently been issued for a smaller car in Long Island City which the gangsters had apparently scrapped.

'Was there anything else taken with the car?' Detective Bruckman asked the doctor.

'Why, yes, my instruments and a can of ether,' Dr Valentine replied.

'Is this the can?' asked Bruckman, holding up the metal cylinder that had been found in Giordano's bag.

The doctor examined the container carefully before giving his response. 'I would say it was. It is exactly like the one that I always carried.'

With that admission, the investigating team had found another vital link in their efforts to solve the crime.

Meanwhile, the results of the various tests that Sergeant Harry Butts of the Ballistics Bureau had carried out on the guns found in Giordano's bag provided the final piece of the jigsaw. The tests proved that the markings on bullets taken from Mullins's body were the same as those fired from one of the revolvers found in Giordano's possession. It now appeared that the police had assembled a watertight case.

The trial of Odierno and Giordano was expedited. On 1 November 1931 the testimony of the eyewitnesses and ballistics experts, as well as the tale of the subterfuges by which the licence plates were obtained for the stolen car, were presented to the jury.

Flying in the face of all gangland codes of conduct, two employees of Stevens and Ahearn – Charles Dingereisser and Peter Westerman – testified against the two gangsters who stood accused of murdering their colleague at the beer-drop. Dingereisser even told the court that he was 'in the beer business', which was still an illegal activity at the time. Another man who testified was Pete Donohue, the Dutchman's 'traffic manager'. All three substantiated the people's contention that the killing was motivated by the dizzy spiral of hate between Dutch Schultz and Mad Dog Coll. They testified that Tuffy Odierno, who had fired the fatal shots, had never even seen Mullins before. They said that he had gone to the garage, called Mullins's name and shot him in cold blood as soon as he appeared.

The trial lasted four weeks, during which time hundreds of thousands of words were entered for the record. In summing up, District Attorney Charles G. McLaughlin, who prosecuted the case, told the jury that the issue at stake was one of law and order versus rule by gangdom. He described Mullins as not a gangster but 'an inoffensive person' who had drifted into the occupation of checking beer kegs.

For his part, former magistrate Albert H. Vitale, counsel for the defence, told the jury that the state had failed to prove its charge of first-degree murder against Giordano and Odierno 'beyond reasonable doubt'. In his summation, which lasted three-and-a-half hours and filled ninety pages, Vitale assailed the identification witnesses produced by the state. He strove to convince the jury that Gill and Carroll were hazy and that they flatly contradicted one another. He also charged the state with having failed to prove the existence of any feud between the Coll and Schultz gangs. He contended that the defendants were being tried for murder on the strength of their reputations as lieutenants of Coll.

The jury received the case at 7.50 pm on the evening of 30 November 1931, had a recess for supper and began its deliberations at 9.30 pm. It took the members of the jury a mere hour and twenty-five minutes to reach their conclusions. Half an hour before the verdict was announced, the jurymen had asked to see one of the two suitcases found in Giordano's room and the revolver and bullets which the prosecution had introduced as evidence in the killing of Mullins. The verdict of the jury was delivered by the foreman to Judge James M. Barrett at 10.55 pm.

On the announcement of a guilty verdict, Tuffy Odierno slumped forwards, as if he had been struck, and burst into tears. He went pale to the lips and sagged visibly as fat, salty tears coursed down his cheeks. The self-proclaimed tough had to be supported by a deputy sheriff as he gave his pedigree. He tremblingly told the court that he was a chauffeur and that he lived at 308 East 154th Street.

His partner took the verdict stolidly and smiled defiantly. He described himself as a 'performer', giving his address as the Maison Hotel.

A couple of days later, on 3 December, Judge Barrett sentenced twenty-year-old Dominick Odierno and thirty-two-year-old Frank Giordano to be executed in the electric chair during the first week of the new year. This was one of the rare cases where gangsters had been found guilty of first-degree murder for the killing of other gangsters. Indeed the pair were the only people ever brought to book during the Coll-Schultz bloodletting. The two men were stunned by the verdict, as recent precedents had lulled them into believing that mobsters were above the law. Plans for a party to celebrate their acquittal were hastily cancelled, as the pair were dispatched to the death-house at Sing Sing. They lingered there while a reprieve was sought through the Court of Appeals. A new trial was denied, and 30 June 1932 was designated as the day of their execution.

Dutch Schultz, the man whom the murder of Mullins had been calculated to hurt most, insisted until the day he died that the wrong men had been convicted. In a rare moment of verbal profligacy, the Dutchman granted an exclusive interview to the *New York Post*'s Isaac McAnally, a staff journalist whom he had come to trust over the years. The interview took place in the Palace Chop House, Newark, in October 1935, a week before assassins' bullets interrupted his dinner there and brought the curtain down on his ignominious career. Why someone as morally corrupt as

Schultz, who had himself acted as judge, jury and executioner on countless occasions, should have felt guilt pangs about an alleged miscarriage of justice is inexplicable. The fact that Giordano and Odierno were both former members of his own gang, that the body of evidence amassed against them was formidable, that they had chosen Mullins as their target in order to strike a blow at the very heart of Schultz's operation and that several of his employees had chosen to testify against them make his crocodile tears all the more baffling. Could it have been that the Dutchman was finally losing the plot? He had elected to reveal all to McAnally because he felt that the *Post* 'might go after it stronger' if he did so. McAnally afterwards professed that the Dutchman was deeply concerned at what had happened to the two assassins.

'I don't say they didn't do a lot of other things,' Schultz said, thumping the table with his fist, 'but they didn't do that job.'

He insisted that the pair could not have committed the murder in the Bronx because they had their hands full elsewhere, having captured two of his own beer-truck drivers from one of his speakeasies under the eyes of an off-duty police sergeant who was tending the bar for him. After the drivers had been released unharmed, they had sworn solemnly to the Dutchman that their captors were none other than Frank Giordano and Tuffy Odierno. According to Schultz, he had sent word to one of the prosecutors at the time of the trial that the District Attorney had bagged the wrong killers and that he could prove this if he was required to.

'I told him,' he said, 'that if he sent those boys to the chair he would never be easy in his conscience again as long as he lived. But nobody ever came around to me.'

When pressed as to why he had not produced the drivers so that the accused pair could beat the rap, Schultz began to waver. 'As a matter of fact,' he stammered, 'when I sent the word I didn't say that I could prove both guys were innocent. I only said that I knew Odierno didn't do it. I always liked Toughy [sic] Odierno. He was an amusing little guy and I felt sorry for him. I didn't give a damn about Giordano.'

He brushed aside any suggestions that Coll's men had also been gunning for him. 'Well that didn't matter,' he said. 'When little Odierno was in the death-house I sent him dough so he could have cigarettes and stuff. Hell, you can't be mad at a guy when he's in that place.'

His interview with McAnally ended on a humorous note. 'Don't forget, when you write your piece,' he told the reporter, 'to split all my infinitives for me.'

One question arises from Schultz's bizarre interview. He was not given to acts of generosity, and the nature of his relationship with Tuffy Odierno is unclear. Do we accept his bona fides or could it be that Odierno provided him with insider information about the comings and goings of the Coll gang?

On the eve of his execution, Frank Giordano made one last desperate attempt to escape execution. He confided to the warden that he had important information about the shooting of Michael Vengelli and that the bullet that killed him had been fired by Vincent Coll.

'I know that's the truth,' Giordano confessed, 'since I drove the car that day – the one Coll was firing from.'

This information was relayed to Governor Franklin D. Roosevelt, who asked the warden to grant a twenty-four hour stay of execution. Having reviewed the new information, however, Roosevelt deemed it to be of no practical importance or consequence and that the two Coll henchmen should meet their fate as appointed. The information was worthless because, by that stage, Vincent Coll was already dead.

11

IN THE DOGHOUSE

The successful conviction of Coll's two henchmen was undoubtedly a massive blow for Coll, as he approached his own date with destiny. He received the news of their sentence of execution morosely from his cell in the Tombs, Lower Manhattan. He was presumably none too impressed, either, with the performance of his counsel, Albert H. Vitale, in defending the duo. Filibusterism and obstructionism seemed to be the main weapons in Vitale's armoury, and neither was likely to endear him to a trial jury or a prosecuting judge. There was also a question of credibility. Vitale had left the judiciary under a cloud. He had often been criticised by the media and reform groups alike during his time on the Bench for his leniency towards gangsters in general – and Arnold Rothstein's operation in particular. It later emerged that Rothstein had once lent him $20,000 for services rendered and that Vitale had $100,000 in a secret bank account that could not be satisfactorily explained. An investigation initiated by the Supreme Court found that he had impaired public confidence in the criminal-justice system when he conferred with Legs Diamond and the Artichoke King in a Harlem nightclub at a time when Diamond was on the lam. A court order eventually forced him from the Bench.

Not surprisingly, then, Coll moved for a change of counsel. On its opening day, 9 December, this trial was adjourned for a week by Judge Corrigan following the withdrawal of Coll's defence counsel, Albert Vitale and Edward Broderick. Coll had another man in mind. He had amassed enough income from his kidnapping activities to avail of the services of the finest defender of the era, Samuel S. Leibowitz.

Leibowitz was broad in the beam, with a rostral face and tobacco-coloured eyes. He was as bald as Dutch cheese, and great wads of fat protruded from his neck. He had earned a reputation as the Clarence Darrow of Prohibition times. With a string of high-profile trials, Leibowitz had exposed the US criminal-justice system as just another exceptionally expensive form of showbiz – an opinion that recent televised cases have done little to dispel. He had championed the causes of Al Capone and the Scottsboro Boys before taking up a career on the Bench, where he gained something of a reputation as a hanging judge. He was also a noted orator, and his high jinks in the courtroom resembled those of John Corcoran in modern times.

Leibowitz was born Samuel Simon Lebeau, the only child in a comfortable Jewish family in Jassy, Moldova. The family emigrated to New York in 1897. As their fortunes soared, the Leibowitzes moved to Brooklyn, where Sam attended high school before graduating from the College of Law at Cornell University in 1915. During his college years, he honed his dramatic and debating skills in the various societies in which he was enrolled. He bucked all convention by choosing a career in criminal law, a field that had hitherto been thought to be the preserve of correspondence-school graduates. Having been rejected for service by the US Marine Corps in 1917, after Congress had declared war on Germany, he sold Liberty Bonds as a way of helping the war effort. Spurned for several months, he eventually married Belle Munves, another Jewish immigrant, in 1919. The couple gave birth to fraternal twin boys and a daughter.

Sam's first client was a penniless drunkard who had broken into a bar and stolen seven dollars and a bottle of whiskey. The lawyer rose quickly through the ranks, however, gaining respect amongst the gangster fraternity by securing the release on a technicality of the likes of Abe 'Kid Twist' Reles, a founding member of Brooklyn's Murder Inc. His reputation was further enhanced amongst them when he successfully defended Al Capone against charges that he had a hand in the murder of three members of the Irish White Hand Gang in a speakeasy in Brooklyn.

Coll's switch from Vitale to Leibowitz was the best decision the impetuous young gangster had ever made. The lawyer proved to be worth every cent of his large fee.

Speaking to me almost seventy years after the events took place, Leibowitz's son, Robert, recalls what his father thought of his young client. Though Sam rarely discussed the details of his cases and never consorted with his clients, Robert remembers the general impression that was conveyed over the dinner table. 'Coll was a very good-looking and charming guy. He was a kind of a dandified individual, full of *amour propre*. My father regarded him as a perfect gentleman,' he told me. Robert Leibowitz said that Coll always protested his innocence.

On the opening day of the trial, 9 December 1931, it

was deemed necessary for four prison guards to escort Frank Giordano from the death-house in Sing Sing to General Sessions Court in Manhattan in Warden Lewis E. Lawes's private car. A precedent was in fact being set, as this was the first time in the history of New York that a person under sentence for one capital offence would stand trial for another. Giordano, it will be recalled, had already, six days earlier, been sentenced to die for the murder of Joe Mullins. A legal wrangle had arisen between the two prosecuting jurisdictions as Manhattan District Attorney Thomas T. C. Crain had wanted the baby-killing trial to precede the Mullins trial but had been beaten to it by Bronx County.

On the opening day of Coll's trial, Jacob Shientag, who had been retained, along with Leibowitz, to replace the withdrawing counsel, appealed for an adjournment until the new year to acquaint himself with the case and to prepare a defence. The presiding judge refused such a long delay but, despite vehement protests from the prosecution, gave the defence another week.

Shientag also moved for a change of venue and for Coll to be tried separately instead of in the company of a condemned man. He argued that a prejudicial atmosphere would prevail in the present venue of Manhattan and that the New York State Penal Law said that a man who had been sentenced to life imprisonment was considered legally dead and therefore could not be tried for another crime. For some peculiar reason, Shientag argued, no such provision existed for someone on death row.

Another good reason to seek a postponement or a change of venue was that the presiding judge was none other than Joseph E. Corrigan, known as the most severe and least compromising of all the city's judges. He would be unlikely to acquit Coll on legal loopholes alone and was therefore to be avoided at all costs.

On 15 December, Judge Corrigan denied Shientag's motions, instead agreeing with the state's contention that important witnesses might disappear if the case did not proceed without delay. In many ways this was a pyrrhic victory for the prosecution, as the defence had hoped that the festive spirit would prevail when the jury would have to come to its decision.

The following day the courthouse once more resembled a fortified camp – a state of siege now de rigueur in the prosecution of gangsters. Coll, who had by now dispensed with his Harold Lloyd glasses and wispy moustache, presented himself in a crisp, bespoke powder-blue suit. His hair had returned to its natural colour and he reportedly appeared self-assured and confident. Giordano, on the other hand, appeared morose and crestfallen, as befitted a man who had just been condemned to the electric chair. Time and again Giordano's lawyers had to grab their client by the sleeve to focus his attention on the proceedings. After all, an acquittal in the Vengelli case was of little or no consequence to him, as his fate had already been decided.

It was apparent from the questions that Leibowitz put to the prospective jurors from the blue-ribbon panel which had been assembled that he would be relying heavily on an alibi. 'If this case should warrant our putting on the stand reputable witnesses, who occupy official positions in a community, to show that Vincent Coll was miles and miles away from the scene of the shooting at the time it occurred, would you accept the testimony of those witnesses at face value?' he enquired.

He also castigated the media for inflaming 'the minds of prospective jurors.' This claim was not without foundation, as Coll had constantly been referred to as a 'killer' and a 'baby-slayer'. For his part, Giordano's attorney, Edward J. Broderick, whom Coll had relieved of his duties days earlier, hinted to the jury that the testimony of policemen, who stood to gain a share of the $30,000 reward if the defendants were convicted, should be taken with a large pinch of salt.

The opening exchanges in the trial were uncharacteristically brief. Assistant District Attorney James T. Neary, who hoped that Coll's conviction would be the swansong of a long and successful career as a state prosecutor, took a mere four minutes to signal his intentions to the jury. He warned the co-accused that he had an eyewitness to the shooting.

'This trial is not the result of public hullaballoo about the slaying of this innocent boy,' he avowed, in tones of utter contempt. 'We want a decision only on strict evidence – and that means first-degree murder!'

Untypically, Leibowitz spoke for only two minutes, declaring that the case was a complete fabrication 'manufactured from whole cloth by unscrupulous persons seeking to share in the $30,000 reward.'

This drew an instant rebuke from Neary, and Judge Corrigan asked Leibowitz whether he was prepared to substaniate his claim. 'I most certainly am!' was the defence attorney's controlled response.

Despite Leibowitz's caustic castigation of the press, all the papers printed in its entirety an official communiqué that Coll had issued through his attorney's offices:

I would like nothing better than to lay my hands on the man who did this – I would tear his throat out. There is nothing more despicable than a man who would harm an innocent child. So far as I am concerned, I am not afraid of the outcome. I can prove I was miles away when this crime was committed. It is a frame-up on the part of my enemies, who have tried many times to assassinate me and have failed. Now they are trying to bring about my death through the law.

Violent threats notwithstanding, this press release, which sought to exonerate Coll in advance of a verdict in the case, was a shrewd manoeuvre in the psychological warfare that was being waged against the jury. The statement suggested that Coll, though clearly no angel, had been the subject of continued police harassment and persecution. The police were determined to put him in an early grave and were prepared to use trumped-up charges as a means of achieving this end.

The prosecution's first important witness was twelve-year-old Florence D'Amello, who had been hit in the shoulder during the Harlem baby-shooting as she ran to protect her cousin, three-year-old Michael Bevilacqua. Some months previously, the New York Society for the Prevention of Cruelty to Children had presented her with the Gold Medal for the Outstanding Act of Child Protection. Coll averted his gaze as the bullet-riddled baby carriage, in which Florence had been pushing her cousin, was presented to the court. The young witness then clapped her hands swiftly to indicate the speed at which the bullets had been fired.

Next to give evidence was another young girl, thirteen-year-old Millie De Fine. She had seen a dark car with two occupants nose its way into the street before slowing and laying down a stream of fire at a man who was loafing about outside the Helmar Social Club. The driver, she claimed, had been hatless, but the man who pulled the trigger had worn a soft felt hat pulled down over his eyes almost to the tip of his nose. He had sat at the rear of the car and his gun had been partly camouflaged with a handkerchief. When asked by Neary if she had been able to identify the killers, Millie tentatively scanned the faces of the co-accused before admitting, in a hushed tone, that she had not seen either of their faces.

Leibowitz proceeded crudely to recreate the scene, using two chairs and the witness stand to represent the edge of the car window. He borrowed a policeman's revolver, unloaded it and asked the young girl to demonstrate how the shooting had occurred. Millie, however, was afraid to touch the gun, so it fell upon Leibowitz himself to do so. During this procedure he accidently pointed the weapon at juror number two, who could barely contain his fury.

'It's not loaded,' Leibowitz shamefacedly apologised.

'Well,' piped up the juror, 'I've heard of people being shot by unloaded guns!'

The attorney then borrowed a hat from his clerk and, following the instructions of the witness, pulled it over his eyes until it was evident to the jurors that the gunman's features had been obscured. Detective Cannon told the court that he had asked Coll why he had dyed his hair, grown a moustache and donned a pair of glasses. The gangster had given him a measured reply. 'For several reasons,' he said.

'The papers said that the police were after me and then there was the opposition.'

Leibowitz cornered Detective Cornelius J. Brown, a ballistics expert, into admitting that the police had recovered some firearms and ammunition belonging to a man named Grimaldi in a search of the top floor of apartment number 215, opposite the place where Vengelli had been killed. Six successive attempts to have this information committed to the record were frustrated, however, by Neary's constant objections, which were sustained by Judge Corrigan.

It was at times like this that it became apparent to those in the courtroom that this case carried a great deal more importance for both parties than a run-of-the-mill assignment. Furthermore, it was obvious that there was no love lost between the two counsels. Could there have been a hint of anti-Semitism on the part of Neary and Corrigan, both of whom openly despised Coll's lawyer? Indeed, on occasion the trial threatened to boil over into a personalised slanging match. At one stage, for example, Neary accused his counterpart of orchestrating a long-faces campaign.

'I object to counsel turning around to look at me with ferocity! With a jury here it won't do! Keep that till after hours!'

'If Mr Leibowitz looks at you with ferocity,' Judge Corrigan said, by way of a reply, 'I cannot help it.'

*

As the trial moved into its sixth day, Coll received the staggering news that his partner in crime had been killed in an Albany flophouse. The bullet had finally been made that could kill Legs Diamond, and the gangland merger had been stalled before it had had time to develop.

On 17 December 1931, Legs had appeared again in the courts, amidst huge publicity, charged on a second count of kidnapping James Duncan and assaulting Grover Parks. A former sheriff of Greene County contradicted Duncan and Parks's testimony and provided an alibi for Diamond. There is also evidence that the gangster bribed some of the jurors, who, despite having been sequestered, were easily got at. A not-guilty verdict was returned. Legs, it was observed, did not register the slightest emotion; it was as though he had been aware of the outcome in advance. A burst of applause came from the gallery as Alice ran to embrace him. The verdict was heralded by the media as a victory for gang law over the law of the land. The dynamics of gang law meant that his acquittal was short-lived, however.

That evening, Legs, accompanied by Alice and Kiki and a number of friends, went to Young's speakeasy, where the celebrations lasted well into the wee hours. Legs did not last the pace, though, and made his excuses around midnight, pretending that he was going to brief some newspaper pals. He and John Storer got a cab to 21 Broeck Street, where Kiki, who had retired an hour earlier, was waiting patiently for him. Three hours later, Diamond emerged, full as a newt, and instructed Storer to take him home. Home was in fact his latest safe house, a threadbare flophouse at 67 Dove Street. Legs was so drunk that Storer had to open the door for him and stuff the key in his pocket. The recently freed man staggered up the stairs and collapsed in a drunken stupor on the single-frame bed.

Minutes later, two men got out of a black sedan that had

been parked, waiting. They climbed the stairs and found Legs asleep in his underpants, oblivious to their presence. They shot him three times in the head at point-blank range. As the attackers rushed down the stairs, the housekeeper, Laura Wood, heard one of the men say that he was going back to finish the job.

'That guy ain't human and it will take a lot to get him for sure,' he stated.

His colleague dissuaded him from such a move and, as the car sped off in the tart December night, Mrs Wood called Alice to give her the bad news. 'My God, Jack, what have they done to you?' Alice screamed. 'They killed my dear Jack! Someone do something!'

The police arrived within minutes, and the doctor pronounced him dead. For more than ten minutes, the police failed to weaken Alice's vice-like grip on the body. She yelled hysterically, 'No! No! You can't have him! He's mine, he belongs to me! Let me stay with Jack!' Then she had miraculously composed herself, and she stunned police as she chillingly told them, 'I didn't do it.'

So who did kill Legs? The inventory of suspects was impressive. Waxey Gordon, Dutch Schultz, Vannie Higgins and Owney Madden all wanted Diamond disposed of for a variety of reasons. Nonetheless, the body of evidence suggests that Alice may well have had the most compelling motive of all. Years of having to share his affection publicly with the svelte and sexy Kiki was bound to have frayed the nerves of Legs's neurotic, petulant wife. It also emerged that Irving Bitz and Salvatore Spitale, two prominent figures in the underworld, had lent Legs a sum amounting to almost $200,000 to establish drug connections in Europe. It had become apparent that Diamond had used this money to subsidise his hedonistic lifestyle.

Although Coll was in custody at the time of Leg's murder, one of his retainers was not above suspicion. During the investigation, the Albany police learned that Fats McCarthy, a member of Vince's gang, had been in town at the time. He had been looking for Legs but did not know his whereabouts. It later transpired that Alice had furnished him with the address of the boarding house as well as the number of the room in which he had slept. He was also evidently aware that Jack would not be guarded by his bodyguards and that the landlady, Mrs Woods, was a feeble old woman. We can be certain that Fats's rendezvous with Legs was unlikely to have been a social one. It should be stated, however, that McCarthy was very much a loose canon: he was not bound by the confines of any one gang. There is no evidence to suggest that McCarthy was acting on the orders of Coll, who had nothing to gain and everything to lose from Diamond's death. Fats was essentially a freelance gun-for-hire and could just as easily have been in the employ of Alice or of Bitz and Spitale.

Coll, in all likelihood, felt little personal emotion towards Legs or grief at his death. The two men were never more than business partners, and their marriage of convenience was probably destined to be no more than a temporary, small arrangement. More worrying, however, was the fact that Diamond was likely to be called upon to substantiate Coll's alibi. On his release from a kidnapping-and-torture charge, Diamond had told reporters that the man from Gaoth Dobhair had nothing to do with Vengelli's death.

'All I can tell you is that Coll was far away at the time,' he had declared.

The press now speculated that Vince's alibi was in tatters. It was thought that his attorney would claim that he had been holidaying with Legs at the time of Vengelli's death and that he had remained upstate after the state troopers' dawn swoop on White's Farm on 19 July, in which half a dozen members of his gang had been arrested.

The following morning, Coll craftily parried questions from the media, denying that he had ever known or worked with Diamond. 'I feel sorry for anyone who is bumped off, especially when a guy is lucky enough to beat a rap – and so soon after acquittal!' he told the *New York American*.

*

The most significant twist in the trial occurred the following day, when the state unveiled its star witness, whom Commissioner Mulrooney had gone to great lengths to keep under wraps. Flanked by three plain-clothes detectives and three court attendants, twenty-seven-year-old George Brecht strode purposefully towards the witness stand. He told the court that he had been ambling down 107th Street on the day in question when he had heard what he assumed to be the backfiring of an engine. When he turned around he noticed a car - all previous eyewitnesses had spoken of two cars - containing five men, two in the front and three in the back. Having worked as a chauffeur for the previous seven years, it was Brecht's professional judgement that the car was cruising at between four and eight miles an hour. Two of the men in the car were firing. One of them, who was sitting in the rear, on the left-hand side, had a pistol, while the man directly in front of him had a shotgun. Asked by the District Attorney if any of the men he had seen were present in the courtroom, Brecht walked over to where the co-defendants were sitting and identified Coll as the man in the rear of the car and Giordano as the one directly in front of him.

Brecht told Neary that he had been in the vicinity at the time of the baby-killing because he had applied for a job at a belt factory at 2060 First Avenue but had been told by the watchman that no vacancies existed at that time. It was patently obvious that Brecht had received a fair amount of instruction before testifying. It was also apparent, however, that his evidence was pitted with lacunae and that he would be like a lamb to the slaughter under the cross-examination of an attorney of the calibre and experience of Samuel S. Leibowitz.

Before long, the attorney got his first taste of blood. Brecht was woolly and vague on the point of when he had last worked. He told the court that he did not want to reveal the identity of the alderman whom he had chauffeured for, as he had a wife and two children, whom he wanted to protect. On further prodding, Brecht grudgingly revealed that the name of his employer was Loman, but he refused to tell where he was from. After a short deliberation, Corrigan ruled that it was not necessary for him to reveal his origins. Sensing that the judge had committed an irreversible error and had displayed a bias against the defence, Leibowitz and Broderick moved for a mistrial. Their motion was denied.

Brecht testified that he had been born in Missouri and that he had come to New York on 12 July with $37 in his pocket and had stayed at the Mills Hotel on Thirty-sixth Street and Seventh Avenue. To sustain his lifestyle, he had accepted a job selling Eskimo Pies from a man called George whom he had met in Battery Park shortly after his arrival in the city. The fact that he had only a few nickels left in his pocket was carefully noted by the defence. He claimed to have sold between 100 and 150 Eskimo Pies over a period of ten days.

During the recess, Leibowitz bought one of the pies. On resumption of the proceedings, he asked Brecht to give a description of the label. Not only was he unable to do so, but it also transpired that he was unaware that it was customary in the trade to use dry ice to keep the pies from melting; it was believed that they would remain hard if they were frozen.

'You are sure that Eskimo Pies are sold or handed out to a customer and all that it has on it is a silver wrapper?' enquired Leibowitz.

'I am,' Brecht replied, a shade too readily.

Coll's lawyer sharpened his talons.

'You are just as positive of that as you are that Vincent Coll was in that car?'

Predictably enough, Neary objected to this line of questioning, and Corrigan sustained the objection. Leibo-witz, however, was undeterred and continued to bait Brecht. In a sustained, rapid-fire cross-examination, he undermined the credibility of the witness by establishing that Brecht was being supported by the NYPD.

'Was that the last job you had in the City of New York?' Leibowitz asked

'Yes, sir,' Brecht replied.

'Who has been supporting you since July.'

'The police department.'

'What?'

'The police department.'

'I suppose you read about the case in the papers, didn't you?'

'No, sir.'

'Did you read about the case in the paper at any time?'

'The night it happened.'

'Did you read about it afterwards?'

'No, sir.'

'Did you read the papers day after day?'

'I do.'

'Didn't you follow it up to see if they caught the men that committed the crime.'

'No, sir.'

'You were not interested?'

'I only read the funny paper.'

'So, if I understand correctly, your story in this case before his honour and these jurymen is that, although you had seen a shooting on 107th Street between Second and Third Avenues, and although you read the papers every day, you paid no attention to what the papers said concerning what developments were in the case.'

'No, sir.'

'You were not interested?'

'I went to the commissioner's office to see him, that's all.'

'You were broke at that time, weren't you?'

'No, sir.'

'You still had two or three nickels that you had the day

before, or had you gotten some money?'

'I had money.'

'Well, you had only two or three nickels on 28 July, when you left for the Battery. That's what you told us before.'

'I never said two or three. I said a few nickels.'

'You know there is a $30,000 reward offered for the conviction of the men that killed that child? You know that, don't you?'

'Yes, I found out recently.'

'How recently?'

'After I seen the police.'

'How much of the $30,000 do you expect to get?'

'None.'

'Where have you been living since 29 July?'

'Nineteen West Thirty-second.'

'What kind of place is it?'

'Hotel.'

'What is the name of the hotel?'

'Aberdeen.'

'Who has paid for your expenses?'

'The police.'

'Gone out to entertainments, too?'

'Yes, sir.'

'Theatres?'

'Yes, sir.'

'Did the police pay for that?'

'Yes, sir.'

'By the way, have you sent any money to your family lately?'

'I sure have.'

'How much?'

'Well, that I could not say.'

'You don't remember?'

'Well, I have got slips.'

'When is the last time you sent any money to your family?'

'Last Saturday.'

'How much?'

'That I do not care to state.'

'Do you think it might endanger your family by giving that information?'

'No, it does not.'

'How much money did you send?'

'Isn't that rather personal?'

'I am asking you – how much did you send?'

'That I do not care to state.'

Judge Corrigan ruled that he should answer the question, however.

'I sent her fifteen dollars.'

'Where did you get the fifteen dollars.'

'The police department.'

'Did you send it every Saturday?'

'Yes, sir.'

'For how many weeks?'

'That, I could not say.'

'Is your memory poor on that?'

'Maybe.'

'When did you first start to send the money?'

'A week after I got my first money.'

'When was that?'

'That I could not say.'

'Is your memory poor on that?'

'No. I do not keep dates, though.'

Though he was visibly shaken and perspiring heavily,

Brecht had still not cracked under the strain. A clammy sweat glazed his forehead as he described to the court how his efforts to see Commissioner Mulrooney himself had been thwarted on three occasions before he eventually secured an interview with him. When he had heard what he had to tell, Mulrooney took Brecht under his wing, and the police had underwritten his expenses ever since.

'You wouldn't talk to any subordinates,' Leibowitz pressed. 'You wanted to see the commissioner himself, so that you could bargain for your part of the reward. You wanted to get all the dough.'

'No, I did not!'

Brecht was unable to tell the court how many windows the murder car had.

'I don't count windows,' he muttered, pathetically. Leibowitz took exception to this.

'The witness should not be so fresh and clever,' he objected.

'Why not set a good example?' Judge Corrigan suggested, amid scenes of great hilarity on the benches of the jury.

Brecht proceeded to testify that he had seen Frank Giordano sitting in the middle of the car holding a gun to his shoulder. The man in the rear of the car, he insisted, had had curly, light-brown hair, had been wearing a blue suit and had been hatless.

The cross-examination volleyed back and forth without making any significant breakthrough. Though Brecht had looked as though he might buckle under the strain of the unremitting grilling, he had thus far evaded the defence lawyer's cleverest traps. His diction may have been poor, but he had by and large spoken clearly and crisply, as befitted a man who had been coached for the previous few months. Leibowitz had observed a chink in his armour, however. Every so often, Brecht had lapsed into speaking out of the side of his mouth with the bare minimum of lip movement, as though he were a ventriloquist. Years of experience practising as a criminal lawyer led Leibowitz to suspect that the prosecution's star witness might have served time in a penal institution, in all probability in one of the states that still enforced a system of silence among inmates.

Coll's lawyer took a shot in the dark.

'I notice that you speak from the corner of your mouth. Is that just a habit?' he probed.

Once again, Neary was incensed at his opponent's style of questioning, and his objection was sustained by the court.

'I want to put another question – don't answer until the District Attorney objects,' Leibowitz sneered. 'Have you gotten that habit at any particular institution or place – the habit of speaking out of the corner of your mouth?' Brecht denied having ever been in prison or on a witness stand before. Leibowitz went on to prove to the court that the belt factory that the witness had claimed to have gone to on the day of Vengelli's murder to seek employment did not exist.

Despite these obvious inconsistencies in his testimony, the fact remained that Brecht had positively identified Coll and Giordano as Vengelli's killers. No amount of badger-baiting on the part of Leibowitz could make him budge an inch on this crucial piece of evidence. Brecht claimed to have remembered Coll in particular because of the deep cleft in his chin.

'I say they are the men,' the witness baldly proclaimed to the jury.

'That's what you came here prepared to say,' Coll's lawyer persisted, 'but isn't it a fact that all you can say now is that you only think they are the men?'

Brecht could barely contain his anger. 'If I thought it, I would not say it was them,' he yelled. 'When I see somebody, I am positive. I identify him.'

'You are not mad, are you?' Leibowitz persevered.

'I ain't mad, no,' Brecht bristled. 'But I hate to be called a liar. That's one thing I hate! I don't go around identifying people for nothing!'

'All you are prepared to say is that they look like the men?' the lawyer suggested, as a last, desperate throw of the dice.

The witness stood firmly by his original statement.

'I said – they are the men!'

Though he had managed to discredit much of Brecht's evidence and had suggested that the witness may have had an unsavoury past, Leibowitz had been unable to shake the core of Brecht's testimony. Certainly some of this testimony threatened to strain the jury's credibility to breaking point, but two days of constant pummelling had failed to make him budge on the fact that he had seen the co-defendants firing indiscriminately in Spanish Harlem on the evening of 28 July. Faced with such overwhelming testimony, the jury's task seemed simple.

But luck was on Coll's side. On the morning of 23 December, as Brecht was concluding his testimony, Joseph Gavin, a probation officer attached to the Brooklyn Society for the Prevention of Cruelty to Children, ambled into Leibowitz's office, claiming that he had important information about Brecht's past. He told William Richter, one of the lawyer's assistants, that he would disclose this information to Leibowitz in the presence of Judge Corrigan and Assistant District Attorney Neary. Sensing a breakthrough, Richter bundled Gavin into a cab and rushed him across the river to the Criminal Courts Building. A few minutes' consultation with Leibowitz was sufficient for the esteemed lawyer to realise the gravity of what Gavin had to say. Leibowitz approached the Bench, and an ashen-faced Judge Corrigan decided that the case would be adjourned until all parties had attended a hastily convened conference in his chambers at 4 pm that afternoon.

The tale that Joseph Gavin had to tell did not make easy listening for the prosecution. He had spent seventeen years working as a probation officer in St Louis and had recognised Brecht as one of his former clients there. Gavin had first come into contact with him in February 1925 when, at the age of seventeen, Brecht had been arrested for 'careless living' and put on probation. The following August Brecht was sentenced to two years in the Missouri State Reformatory for stealing two diamond rings from a St Louis jeweller. While awaiting trial, he was accused by a baker of handing him a counterfeit cheque to the value of twelve dollars. He was paroled the following spring but was soon in trouble again.

Between 1926 and 1928 he had been convicted of grand larceny and on one occasion had been sent to a mental institution for observation. In May 1927, he had been the state's main witness in the murder trial of two members of the infamous 'cuckoo gang'. Brecht claimed to have seen Louis Mandel and Lee Orlando leaving the office of Dr August H. Santé, with smoking guns, shortly after the renowned physician's murder. Brecht had positively identified both men but was found to have perjured himself in the witness stand, and the two gangsters had been acquitted. He had been charged with violating his parole a few months later but had escaped censure because, having just turned nineteen, he had been technically too old for probation.

When he was summoned to the judge's chambers, the state's star witness surprised all present. On recognising the probation officer, Brecht greeted him with an all-consuming smile. 'Hello, Mr Gavin,' he said, heartily. 'How are you?' He then admitted to the story Gavin had told of his previous court experiences.

Judge Corrigan was enraged by this incredible turn of events. In one fell swoop, his hard-earned reputation as the nemesis of gangland had been rendered redundant by a recidivist perjurer.

The following day, Christmas Eve 1931, Brecht was recalled by the defence and forced to admit his flawed pedigree and the fact that he had lied under oath about his criminal past the previous day. Dispatches from St Louis revealed a startling similarity between his eyewitness account of the St Louis homicide and the Spanish Harlem massacre. In both instances, he had been 'just bumming around', he said, and the day after the murders he had gone to the police and told of having been an eyewitness, adding that he could identify the murderers. Several of the jurors, obviously astonished at the turn the testimony had taken, engaged in intense whispered discussions as Brecht's admissions were prised out of him.

He had been so thoroughly discredited that Leibowitz rested, without calling any witnesses, and offered to give the case to the jury immediately, without summation. He had hoped that the jury would decide Coll's fate on the night before Christmas, but Corrigan was wise to his machinations and sent the jury home. The case was adjourned until 28 December.

As Giordano left the courthouse, flanked by his armed guard, he shouted across to Neary, 'A very merry Christmas to you and your family!'

'The same to you and your friend Coll,' was Neary's seasonal response. Behind the superficial festive cheer, however, he must have realised that he had presided over one of the great legal cock-ups of his time.

Any hopes that he may have harboured that the perjury of the star witness would be forgotton over the holiday period proved unfounded. In the Christmas Day edition of the *Daily News* it was reported that the five-man bodyguard that had been protecting the prosecution's star witness had been withdrawn:

> The reason is that gangland is laughing up its well-tailored sleeves instead of plotting vengeance against the 'mystery witness'.

A cautionary note was sounded for Coll in the *Sunday News*, however, lest he should lose the run of himself:

> Meanwhile the underworld buzzed with reports that Coll, like his friend the late Jack 'Legs' Diamond, would be put on the spot if freed.

Coll, who spent a quiet Christmas in Murderer's Row of the Tombs, was jubilant at the news. Giordano, however, was reported to be indifferent to it.

Though the result of Coll's murder trial now seemed like a foregone conclusion, the prosecution was divided as to what course of action they would pursue next. Sensing a hornet's nest, District Attorney Thomas T. C. Crain urged Neary to see the trial through to the end and let the jury decide thereafter. Vincent Coll was a lawless psychopath who lived in a depraved world of violence and brutality, he argued, and society as a whole would thank Neary for sending him to the chair, even if the course of justice had been perverted in the process. But Neary would have none of it and threatened to resign rather than secure a conviction on the strength of the testimony of a perjurer.

Crain panicked and tried to wash his hands of the debacle, which had so far cost the exchequer around $60,000. He passed the buck, declaring that Brecht had been Mulrooney's 'private witness'. Mulrooney also passed the buck. Though he initially refused to comment on the case, as it was still sub judice, he later emphatically denied that his department had had any prior knowledge of Brecht's disreputable past. He initiated an inquiry on St Stephen's Day on the suspicion that a minor police official had been derelict in his duty by concealing the criminal and mental-deficiency record of the state witness. The report of the investigation attempted to put a reasoned gloss on the events. In his overeagerness to prosecute Coll, a minor police official withheld the information from his superiors and the District Attorney's Office, according to the report's findings. Stenographic records of Brecht's original story to the police were conveniently unavailable. Mulrooney's stolid stonewalling made for poor copy; he could not fool all of the people all of the time.

When the trial resumed on 28 December, Neary was

clear about what had to be done. With an air of resignation, he rose and addressed the court.

'In view of the fact that this witness has lied on the stand about his former convictions,' he said, 'I now appear before you, sir, and in the interests of justice I move the discharge of these defendants.'

Neary's move for a directed verdict of acquittal shocked the court. Nobody, including Coll, had thought that he would cave in so easily. News had been relayed to him from St Louis, however, suggesting that Brecht's criminal record was even more crowded than had at first been anticipated. Coll cradled his chin as his eyes flashed with pleasure. Giordano, despite the death sentence hanging over him, seemed no less pleased.

In directing the verdict, Judge Corrigan went to great lengths to exculpate the police and the prosecutor for producing a witness whose credibilty was now shattered.

'This is a most extraordinary case,' he stated. 'There is no doubt in my mind that both the District Attorney and the police were honest and fair throughout. Police Commissioner Mulrooney took a great interest in the case, and he had Brecht put to as many tests as possible, even having him examined by a doctor as to his sanity. But the wisest men may be fooled sometimes.

'Brecht made a good impression on me on the witness stand, as he stood under several hours of severe cross-examination. He also gave an excuse for what I thought was his first and only lie, but from his record, as read by Mr Neary, that appears not to have been his only lie.'

The judge then addressed the jury. 'It is important, I think, not only for you gentlemen, but for the community

Bugsy Siegel: he thwarted Coll's plan
to murder Lucky Luciano.

Legs Diamond: the clay pigeon of the underworld.

A rogues' gallery, members of Coll's gang pictured after being taken into custody: Tuffy Odierno, Mike Basile, Pasquale del Greco, Frank Giordano and Vincent Coll.

A delighted Vincent Coll shakes the hand of Samuel Leibowitz
after his acquittal on the Harlem baby massacre charge.
To the left of the picture is Raymond J. Riley,
who also represented Coll. (Corbis Bettman)

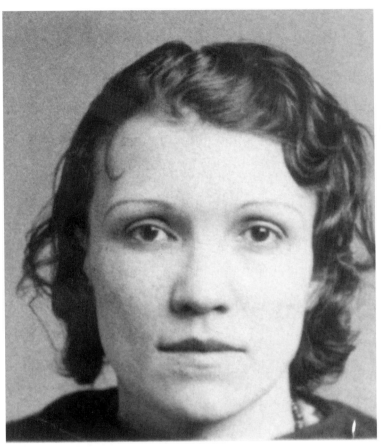

Lottie Coll, an underworld Bermuda Triangle: men who were
associated with her vanished off the face of the earth.

Bo Weinberg: did he kill Vincent Coll?

The body of Vincent Coll is removed from the New London
Pharmacy, West 123rd Street, New York, on 8 February 1932.

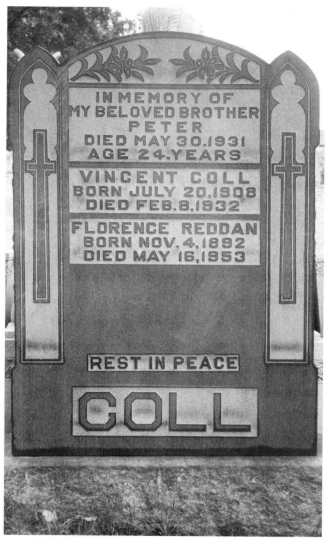

IN MEMORY OF
MY BELOVED BROTHER
PETER
DIED MAY 30.1931
AGE 24.YEARS

VINCENT COLL
BORN JULY 20,1908
DIED FEB.8,1932

FLORENCE REDDAN
BORN NOV.4,1892
DIED MAY 16,1953

REST IN PEACE

COLL

Vincent Coll's grave at St Raymond's Cemetery,
the Bronx, New York.

Walter Winchell: the legendary hack predicted Coll's death
a couple of hours before he was murdered. (Hal Layer)

Lottie receives a sentence of six to twelve years for the manslaughter
of Millie Schwartz. Beside her in the dock
stand Joseph Ventre and Alfred Guarino.

at large, to understand that the courts are just as much interested – and the District Attorney's Office, and the police department – in seeing that justice is done as any individual can be. We do not sit here to get convictions. We sit here to try and ascertain the truth, no matter which way that truth may point. If a man is guilty, he should be convicted. If he is innocent, he should be acquitted. That is the spirit of our law, and it certainly is the spirit in which this court is administered.'

The judge paused to regather his thoughts. The tension was unbearable, particulary for Coll.

'The court, the District Attorney and the police are only interested in seeing justice done,' he announced, finally, 'and in view of the facts in this case I direct you to return a verdict of not guilty.'

Corrigan's parting shot brought the curtain down on the trial of the People versus Vincent Coll and Frank Giordano, which had lasted seven days in total. Both men were declared not guilty of the charge against them.

12

DOG UNLEASHED

Following the remarkable outcome of their trial, neither Coll nor Giordano was set free. Giordano returned to his cell in the death-house in Sing Sing pending the outcome of his appeal against the Mullins verdict, which was of course unsuccessful. For his part, Coll was given no time to revel in his new-found freedom. He was immediately turned over to the Bronx authorities on charges arising from the Sheffield Farm depot hold-up in 1928 and the Sullivan Law charge, on which he had jumped bail. He was remanded to the Tombs by Judge Corrigan.

As he was being led to the courtroom, he waved to Lottie and his sister Florence, who were sitting beside each other towards the back of the building. Lottie, who had turned out in cardinal red for the occasion, blew him kisses.

'I'll be seeing you, baby,' Coll promised her.

Coll's acquittal was not totally unexpected, however, and he had prepared a statement to cover such an eventuality. He delivered this statement with aplomb to the press on the steps of the courthouse before being whisked away to the Bronx.

'I have been charged with all kinds of crimes,' he told

the attentive hacks, 'but baby-killing was the limit. I am glad a jury has vindicated me, but I owe more than I can ever pay to Mr Leibowitz and Mr Riley.' [Raymond J. Riley was Leibowitz's co-counsel.]

The *Daily News* ran a picture of Coll's toothsome smile of victory and described him as 'carefree, affable and gay'.

Shortly after being acquitted of the Harlem baby-killing, Coll appeared before Justice Salvatore Cotillo in the Bronx. Assistant District Attorney Soleman Boneparth asked that bail be fixed at the astronomical figure of $50,000 due to the fact that Coll had jumped the $10,000 bail that had been set for him the previous July. Leibowitz protested that such an excessive figure violated his client's constitutional rights. He described the Sheffield Farm charge as 'as big a fraud and fake as the murder charge' and said that Coll would gladly face trial in the morning provided the jury were not all ringers. If anybody knew about ringers it was Leibowitz, the District Attorney countered. Coll's counsel took great exception to this, and Judge Cotillo adjourned the hearing until New Year's Eve to ward off any ugly scenes.

Three days later, Vincent Coll left the Bronx Supreme Court a free man. He owed his release to a writ of habeas corpus obtained by his attorney on the day of his acquittal. The writ was argued on 31 December 1931 before Justice Cotillo, who held Coll on $50,000 bail on the Sheffield Farm charge and fixed $10,000 bail on the Sullivan Law charge. A personal bond without collateral was posted by the Lennox Bonding Company and had effectively been set up by Schultz and Madden. Both men wanted Coll out in the open, where he would make an easy target – a fact that was not lost on Coll. 'I didn't know the boys cared,' he was reported to have said.

During his trial he had confided to John Capozucca, Leibowitz's sidekick, that he expected to be bumped off sooner rather than later. 'Johnny, I know if I ever beat this rap, I'm gonna get it. But before I go, I swear to Christ, I'm gonna take at least fifteen more of them bastards,' he told him.

The first person Coll greeted as he left the clerk's office in the courtroom was his girlfriend, Lottie. He draped his gauzy arms around her shoulders and gave her a fervent hug and a kiss. Then he turned to his sister, Florence, and her husband, Joe, and shook their hands firmly. He told the waiting press that he planned to celebrate New Year's 'somewhere in the country' with relatives and friends.

The courthouse was in the heart of Dutch Schultz's fiefdom, and Coll was urged to leave the court by a side door. 'Nothing doing,' he said, as he led the way to the street. The party then sped away in a waiting sedan.

*

Meanwhile, reaction to the Brecht debacle was stinging. Public indignation ran high. The *Daily Mirror*'s editorial was in no doubt where the blame lay:

> Collapse of the prosecution in the Coll murder case seems to indicate an extraordinary condition of incompetence in the District Attorney's Office.
>
> The state's star witness, Brecht, whose testimony had been counted on to convict Coll of an atrocious murder, proves at the last minute an utterly untrustworthy individual with a police record of his own,

and the case, built on his testimony, is summarily thrown out of court by way of an instructed not-guilty verdict.

If anything like proper precaution had been observed by Mr Crain's staff in establishing the character of the witness, no such ridiculous and costly fiasco would have been possible. The defence maintains Brecht's record was in police hands long before he appeared on the witness stand to identify Coll as the Harlem baby-killer but that, for certain reasons, it did not reach Crain.

If this be true, it implies on the part of the police authorities something worse than inefficiency, but whatever explanation may be offered, there is no excuse for failure of the prosecution to obtain information as to Brecht through resources of its own.

The police's incompetence was perceived as the latest in a long list of blunders. The evidence against Coll was extremely flimsy and had been cobbled together from a mass of disjointed and unrelated fragments. Borrowing a phrase from the Great War, the *Herald Tribune* described the fiasco as 'bad staff work'. The *Sun* went one further in its editorial on 29 December:

In directing a verdict of acquittal in the case of a man accused of murder, Judge Corrigan took pains yesterday to exculpate the police and the District Attorney's Office from suspicion of conspiracy to swear away the life of the accused.

So highly is Judge Corrigan regarded that his

certificate of character will win popular acceptance.

The prosecution was merely dumb.

Brecht himself had been committed to Bellevue Hospital and the Neurological Institute by Judge Corrigan for observation. He was released a fortnight later, as the hospital authorities had deemed him to be in complete control of his faculties. When the case against Coll had collapsed, Leibowitz had asked the court to commit him for perjury.

'That's a matter for the court to decide,' Judge Corrigan had snarled. 'The court will mind its business and prefers that you mind yours!'

Most commentators took the line that the prosecution had been incompetent and negligent and had attempted to abort the course of justice by framing the suspects on the perjured evidence of an inveterate liar with a criminal past. Other, more discerning observers started to ask other questions, however.

Three prominent socialist leaders demanded that Governor Roosevelt investigate the show trial thoroughly. In a letter to the governor, Norman Thomas, chairman of the socialist public-affairs committee, Louis Waldman, state chairman of the party, and attorney Charles Solomon asserted that the acquittal of Coll and Giordano indicated 'almost incredible negligence or a deliberately criminal frame-up' by the police. The letter's authors demanded an investigation by a special grand jury. They contended that, if the police had been unaware of the witness's character, they were at the very least negligent, and that if they were aware of it, their conduct was such as to assist rather than convict the defendants. Socialism, however, was not a very popular credo in America at the time, and Roosevelt chose to ignore the request.

More damning perhaps was the fact that Neary – who emerged from the debacle with his reputation in tatters but his honour intact – called for a full-scale investigation of the case by the grand jury. District Attorney Crain peremptorily vetoed him, however.

Meanwhile, other, more bizarre theories were doing the rounds. Some suggested that Coll himself had planted Brecht on the prosecution, an opinion that did not merit serious consideration. Another supposition was that Brecht had been planted by Coll's enemies, of which there were legions. This idea credited the underworld with rather more intelligence than it deserved. They were above the law and would not have dreamed of resorting to it as a means of getting rid of an opponent. Nor would they have relied on as weak a character as Brecht when an 'eyewitness' with an unimpeachable past would have been more reliable. They, of all people, would have known about his criminal background. But why let the facts get in the way of a good, old-fashioned conspiracy theory! Some even went so far as to say that the Syndicate had palmed off Brecht on the unsuspecting police in order to get Coll freed so that he could be disposed of once and for all.

Several years later, Neary broached the subject with Big Frenchy De Mange after bumping into him on the street. De Mange brushed off any suggestion that either he or Madden would have planted such 'an unreliable jerk', as he described him. He did not believe that the Dutchman would have placed his faith in Brecht either.

Another unfounded hypothesis was that the Jimmy Hines

administration in Tammany Hall needed to secure a high-profile underworld conviction to ward off allegations emerging from the Seabury investigation that it was unwilling to tackle gangster violence because it had been bought. Any such suggestions could be refuted if Coll had been convicted.

The story that held the greatest credence on the street, however, involved the complicity of half a dozen of the police's top brass. These officers, it was claimed, had a vested interest in one of the most profitable speakeasies on the East Side; this speakeasy also operated as a pay-off station for gangsters. The previous spring, Coll had employed one of his favourite tactics, brazenly announcing that he was cutting himself in with a 50 per cent shareholding and that his accountants would inspect the books the following morning. This left the police officers with a sticky dilemma. They knew that, if they refused to give him what he had asked for, Coll had the wherewithal to open up a Pandora's box of police graft. They finally acceded to his demands, with the caveat that they would ensure that this jumped-up whippersnapper would get his comeuppance sooner rather than later. George Brecht provided them with an opportunity to do just that.

Coll himself was jubilant, and if he got wind of the various stories that were circulating, he paid no heed to them. His delight and relief were unbounded, and he was determined to make up for lost time. Three months is a long time in organised crime, though, and the underworld hierarchy that he had hoped to re-enter on his release had altered considerably in his absence. His standing had atrophied during his protracted stay as a guest of the nation, and the Syndicate had tightened its grip on the criminal world.

Besides, Coll's operation was in tatters. Two of his top aides, Frank Giordano and Dominic Odierno, were soon to walk their last mile, to the electric chair. Fats McCarthy had fled upstate and his underworld ally Legs Diamond was dead. On top of this, Coll's coffers were empty. Though he had undoubtedly received his money's worth from Leibowitz, the country's top defence counsel did not come cheaply.

Vincent was as good as his word, however. On 1 January he called to the lawyer's Brooklyn office and deposited a brown paper bag, containing several thousand dollars, on his desk. 'Here's your dough, Uncle Sam,' he was reported to have said.

Leibowitz saw him to the door. Both men were unaware, however, that they had narrowly escaped an assassin's bullets. Some years later, Abe 'Kid Twist' Reles, one of the most-feared mobsters in New York, confided that he had gone to Leibowitz's offices in Court Street that day to kill Coll. Reles was the top hit man of Murder Inc, an organisation to which the Syndicate subcontracted its dirty work. Reles had followed Coll to the office and lay in waiting in the crowded street, ready to ambush him. He was just about to draw when he spotted a policeman loping leisurely down the street. Reles later confessed that he had been sure of nailing Coll but 'in a deal like that, maybe a coupla shots go haywire, an' the counsellor would of got clipped too. So there'd of been one mouthpiece less.'

The irony of this was that Reles himself owed the fact that he could roam the streets, killing rival gangsters, to the 'mouthpiece' in question. Leibowitz had secured his release from an armed robbery charge in 1928 by persuading the jury that a signed confession had been obtained under duress. In this context, Reles would certainly have had to take out his former counsel on the basis that he would have recongised him as the assailant.

The Kid himself later achieved notoriety when he agreed to turn state's evidence against his colleagues in Murder Inc. On the morning of 12 November 1941, the day he was due to give testimony, Reles's broken body was found five storeys below his room at the Half Moon Hotel in Coney Island. He had tied two bed-sheets together and had apparently tried to escape out of his window. The fact that he was wearing a grey sweater and a cap that had not been in his wardrobe the previous day alerted many to the fact that all was not as it appeared. The Brooklyn prosecutor Burton B. Turkus, known to the mob as 'Mr. Arsenic', doubted that Reles could have plummeted to his death 'from the centre of a guard that would have made the crown jewels safe in Jesse James's parlour.' Two official investigations – and several books – later, the cause of Reles's death remains a mystery. Neither has it been determined whether he committed suicide or was defenestrated. It was noted with some pleasure in mob circles at the time, though, that the canary could sing but could not fly.

*

Coll, oblivious to the fact that Reles had tried to eliminate him, had other things on his mind. On 4 January 1932 he and Lottie obtained a licence to marry in the Municipal Building. Both gravely gave their pedigree to the un-suspecting clerk but were slightly economical with the truth in some of the finer details recorded on their sworn affidavit – which Coll completed with immaculate penmanship. He gave his place of residence as the Hotel New Yorker, while she said that she lived at 347 West Thirty-ninth Street. Coll was not registered in the hotel, however, and the address given by Lottie was in fact an office building in the garment centre. Vincent, who described himself as a twenty-three-year-old bricklayer, recorded the names of his father and mother as well as the fact that he had been born in Donegal. His partner discarded the name of Lottie Kreisberger for that of Charlotte Von Denninger, her maiden name, which was understandable under the circumstances, as she testified that this was to be her first marriage. Always one for lofty airs, she registered herself as a model and gave her age as twenty-four, an extremely conservative estimate. Once the marriage licence had been granted, the couple sped off in their sedan. Attempts by the media to trace them over the following few days proved futile, and even Coll's closest friends maintained that the news of the impending marriage was a complete surprise to them. They were believed to have gone to Albany.

The granting of a licence to marry does not necessarily mean that the couple were wed, however, and, contrary to what was reported at time, there is some doubt as to whether the couple ever got married. Shortly after the Gaoth Dobhair man's premature death, Commissioner Mulrooney asked Lottie when she had married Coll, but he received no answer. No return had ever been made of the licence issued on 4 January 1932. On top of this, Vince's sister, Florence, always maintained that he had never been married. His death certificate would seem to add weight to this assertion, listing him as single. At the time of Vincent's death, Florence informed the police that Lottie's declaration that she was the legal wife of her brother was false. Lottie denied this, however. 'That's not fair, we are married. We were married in Albany. We got a new licence there,' she told the *Daily News*.

It is entirely conceivable that the couple had planned to get married but had not got around to doing so before Vincent was mowed down, just over a month later. As his funeral ceremony suggested, the delay may well have been due to the difficulty in getting a Catholic priest to preside over the marriage ceremony.

In Celtic times, wedding celebrations lasted for a year and a day, and if the couple had indeed never married they gave a good impression of having done so, renting out the honeymoon suite in the Lexington Hotel. The reasonable assumption is that they were at the very least common-law husband and wife.

Their 'honeymoon' serenity was rudely shattered, however, on 11 January, when they were arrested on charges that they had put aside their supposed newly acquired wedding bliss to continue their criminal activities. The couple were seized after detectives had overheard one of Coll's henchmen give a succint but suggestive message. Having returned from Albany earlier that day, Vincent, Lottie and Mike Basile stopped outside a cigar shop at Fifty-eighth Street and Lexington, where the latter went into a phone booth to relay a message to Louis Bifano, another member of the gang. The police had put a tail on Vince, though, and Detective Kiser listened in to Basile's conversation, which consisted of one sentence only: 'The boss says tell the boys "be ready for tonight".'

The triumvirate were immediately arrested on the strength of Basile's cryptic remark – a clear signal to Coll that he should give telephone booths the widest of berths in the future. The results of the police's trace helped locate Bifano, who was arrested and taken to the East Fifty-first Street Station, where he joined his three colleagues. Down at the station, Coll flashed a bankroll of $500, peeled off a few bills and ordered sandwiches, coffee and cigarettes all round. Impeccably groomed, he and Lottie presented a natty appearance in what was presumed to be their wedding raiment. In the space of a week their occupations had changed considerably: he was now a 'clerk' and she a 'housewife'. They gave their address as 1465 Jessup Avenue, the Bronx – Florence's house.

The police questioned the prisoners for several hours without obtaining any useful information. The investigation disclosed, however, that Bifano had made several calls after he had received Basile's message. In view of these calls, the police believed that the four arrests had prevented, for the present, some major operation that had been planned by the Coll gang. The implication was that the job that the boys had to 'be ready for' was the liquidation of the Dutchman. The holding of the four was justified on these grounds, even though it was admitted unofficially that the conspiracy charge against Coll and Basile should have been backed up with additional corroborating evidence.

In addition to the charge of acting in concert to commit a crime, Bifano was booked for violation of the Sullivan Law. The Bronx detectives who had arrested him had found a loaded pistol beside his bed. He was held on bail of $2,500. Coll remained in a cell, but Lottie and Basile, both of whom were charged with violation of the Sullivan Law and conspiracy to commit a crime – although neither had a gun – were released on $10,000 bail each by Magistrate Benjamin Greenspan in night court. Called upon once more to perform heroics, Samuel Leibowitz told the court that he would have this 'silly charge thrown out the window by morning'.

'That remains to be seen,' Magistrate Greenspan retorted, sourly.

The following morning the charge was indeed thrown out of the window. Leibowitz stated that he would apply to the Supreme Court to obtain bail for Coll. He referred to the arrests as a 'preposterous attempt to frame Coll.'

The gangster himself was incensed over the round-up and told Inspector Sullivan as much, in no uncertain terms. Coll answered questions sulkily. When the inspector wanted to know what he had been doing with a pistol, Coll replied, 'I have no gun; I don't know anything about a gun.'

'Well then,' Inspector Sullivan suggested, 'the gun your friend had.'

'What friend?' snapped Coll.

'One of the men arrested with you,' Sullivan said, probing further.

'I don't know them at all,' the mobster said, by way of a reply. 'Ask them if they know me. I don't know them.'

Meanwhile, the detectives who were keeping a close watch on the house where Bifano had been seized noticed a familiar figure approaching the building at midnight. It was Patsy Del Greco, who had been amongst those taken in during the original round-up of the Coll gang on 4 October 1931. He had been released only a short time before from the workhouse, where he had served two months for violation of the recently introduced law on association with criminals. He offered no resistance when detectives approached him. He was taken to Westchester Police Station and charged with being implicated in a recent hold-up of a drugstore.

The morning after his arrest, Coll was brought before Magistrate Bernard Mogilesky in West Farms Court, but the charge was dismissed due to lack of evidence. Telling the boys 'to be ready for tonight' hardly constituted proof that he was about to commit a crime.

The charge of 'conspiracy to commit crime', on which he was arraigned, was a slim one that was doomed to failure, but it served notice to Coll that the New York Police Department was determined to drive him and his gang out of town. If they could not pin a charge on him, they would instead harass him constantly so that his life would not be worth living. They were still smarting from the lingering hurt of the collapse of the Vengelli trial, which had been regarded publicly as a damning indictment of the way in which the department went about its daily business. The young gang chieftain received confirmation to that effect shortly before the hearing.

'We're going to pick you up again,' Assistant Chief Inspector John J. Sullivan told Coll. 'We're going to continue to pick you up until we drive you out of the city.' As an afterthought, the inspector added, 'But we really ought to leave you here so that people can see the baby-killers.'

Coll became apoplectic with rage. 'Baby-killers?' he roared, in knotted fury. 'I'm no baby-killer.'

He then launched into a verbal attack on the way in which the authorities were harassing Lottie. The *New York Evening Post* ran the headline 'Coll is Warlike Defending

Wife'. 'Why don't you people leave her alone,' he was reported to have shouted at a poker-faced Sullivan.

Two days later Coll found himself an unwilling guest of the police once again, when detectives, apparently acting under instructions to take him into custody on sight, closed in on him and his 'bride' at Eighth Avenue and Forty-ninth Street, questioned him for two hours at the West Forty-seventh Street Station and then released him. He showed signs of exasperation when Acting Captain Patrick F. McVeigh and other detectives of the headquarters office confronted him at two o'clock in the afternoon as he and Lottie emerged from a restaurant in Madison Square Gardens. He was curtly told not to 'get tough' and was driven in his blue Buick sedan to the station house. Satisfied that the new car did indeed belong to Coll, the detectives took note of the number of its motor and other parts and examined three handbags, which were found to contain only clothing. He was strip-searched and questioned for over two hours. At 4 pm, when the precinct policemen detailed to the 4 pm-to-midnight tour of duty were lined up in the station house for roll-call, Vincent and Lottie were allowed to leave. As they brushed their way past the patrolmen, they refused to say where they were going.

'I don't like bein' annoyed this way!' he bellowed.

Two days later, on 16 January 1932, the young mobster found himself once again in the clutches of the law, this time to answer the charges on which he had been released on bail – the Sheffield Farm heist and the Sullivan Law rap, for which his bail surety had been forfeited. He was arraigned before another familiar figure, Judge James M. Barrett, whom he had appeared before as a teenager and who had recently condemned Giordano and Odierno to death. While he was waiting to be called before the Bench, he listened with mocking contempt to the judge as he harangued a teenager about the futility of pursuing a career in crime – before handing him a three- to five-year suspended sentence. When his own name was called, he sidled over to the judge, held his gaze provocatively and pretended to spit in his face.

In view of the three years that had elapsed since the heist had taken place, the District Attorney requested an indefinite postponement to give the state time to round up potential witnesses, as some of them had died or moved to another state in the intervening years. Leibowitz protested that they would all be 'old men' before the book of evidence was produced. Coll's spitting performance had backfired, however, and Judge Barrett granted the request. As he was leaving the building, Lottie ran ahead of him and peered up and down the street for members of the opposition who might want to take a pot-shot at him.

Though he might have been expected to buckle under the strain of Mulrooney's war of nerves and campaign of victimisation, Coll was in fact on a comeback trail. There was some evidence that, despite – or maybe because of – his reputation, he had managed to recruit some new goons. There were daily raids on the Dutchman's speakeasies and beer-drops. Some of his garages had been bombed and many of his trucks were hijacked, and their cargo flogged at cut-rate prices to his competitors. All of these tactics bore the hallmarks of the Mad Dog – a fact that had not escaped Schultz, who promptly returned to his state of effective house arrest after a brief taste of liberty during Coll's period in custody. Schultz also resumed his acquaintance with Polly

Adler's whores off Fifth Avenue. On 21 January, the *Daily News* ran a lead that suggested that the Coll-Schultz vendetta had become so out of hand that the authorities were powerless to control it. The piece, which was penned by Arthur James Pegler, one of America's top crime reporters, made grim reading:

Two desperate gun mobs, becoming daily more reckless in their battle for booze authority, are keeping the entire police department on guard day and night to prevent a conflict of unparalleled ferocity . . . Evidence in police possession of the increasingly menacing situation involving the Schultz and Coll gangs is causing disquietude in official circles. Those in charge of plans to keep them apart say if they ever meet there will be a mob massacre far worse than Chicago's Valentine's Day affair.

What the police know is that Schultz, in deadly fear of Coll, remains day and night in hiding from the latter's band of assassins, which includes fifteen of the most desperate killers in the continent. The Schultz defence force also includes well-known desperadoes, but they, as well as their boss, don't want any part of Coll's men if they can avoid an encounter.

Coll boasts he has Schultz on the run and also that his followers intend to clean up all opposition in Manhattan, the Bronx and Brooklyn to his own supremacy in the liquor traffic.

Detectives detailed on the difficult job of herding fifty or more armed killers say Schultz's gunnery experts are afraid to go into battle with Coll's sharpshooters. Numerous instances have been reported wherein the Coll raiders have wrecked speakeasies under Schultz control while Schultz armed guards stood by unresisting.

One authority said last night, 'Coll is as dangerous as a mad dog. He is probably the most dangerous man in this country today. Obviously, the police cannot ally themselves with one band of criminals to protect the other. The best that can be done is to maintain constant watch over both mobs and round them up when an overt act is committed.'

There is well-founded apprehension, however, that when the battle between Coll and Schultz gunmen takes place it will break so quickly as to endanger innocent lives before police can reach the scene of the conflict. That is why hundreds of uniformed and plainclothes men are being kept constantly on the trails of Coll and his Bronx quarry.'

Pegler's talk of a slaughter on the scale of the Valentine's Day Massacre in Chicago turned out to be a self-fulfilling prophecy. Coll's 'honeymoon' call to arms was answered at 9.40 pm on 1 February 1932. Two cars, each carrying four men, halted outside 1216 Commonwealth Avenue. The street is now a quiet, leafy Bronx suburb, and the spacious, red-brick house is owned by a large family who are unaware of its bloody past. On that particular spring evening two masked men from each car entered the building and mounted the stairs to the second floor of the two-family dwelling. Inside the apartment, more than a dozen adults were about to sit down to a game of cards when they were startled by an unexpected ring at the door. One of five children at play in the apartment ran to the portal and threw it open. Immediately there was a withering blast from four heavy-calibre pistols as the four gunmen burst in with guns blazing, mowing down their victims before they had a chance to defend themselves or dive for cover. Some of the men and women were seated at the dinner table, while others stood by their chairs. With the first volley of bullets, the scene of the festivities was turned into pandemonium, the shouts of the panic-stricken children rousing the neighbourhood. The invaders, having caught their enemies by surprise, emptied their pistols, which the police later learned were automatic weapons of .38 and .45 calibre, fled downstairs, jumped into their cars and sped away. They had completed their task in barely a minute. In the adjacent flat, Joseph Parrone, the deaf and aged father of one of the occupants of the apartment, slept peacefully throughout the shooting.

One of the boys – as yet unschooled in the ways of gangland – who had been playing in the apartment ran up to Patrolman James Welsh in white-faced excitement, crying. The policeman, who had been passing Westchester and Commonwealth Avenues as part of his nightly beat, was informed that 'men were shooting upstairs'. Welsh reached the flat a few minutes after the gangsters had fled and found a veritable bloodbath. On the floor in a pool of gore lay the perforated bodies of Patsy Del Greco, Coll's top retainer; Fiore Basile, an ex-convict and brother of Mike; and Emily Torrizello. The gunmen had apparently concentrated their fire on Del Greco and Basile. On his death certificate, Del Greco was described as a painter, while Basile was said to have been a peddler. The chosen occupations of gangsters never ceases to amaze!

The unusual procedure of performing an immediate autopsy of the three dead persons was adopted, in order to determine what kind of bullets had been fired. Four bullets were found in Basile's body, while Del Greco had been hit three times. A single gunshot to the head had killed Torrizello, the wife of a Bronx businessman, who had jumped into the line of fire to protect either Basile or Del Greco.

Three other people were injured in the raid and were rushed to the Fordham Hospital. Louis Basile, brother of Mike and Fiore, was wounded over the heart and in the left arm. Their sister, the recently widowed Mrs Lena Vinciguerra, was hit in the jaw, while nineteen-year-old Joseph Parrone, who had just 'dropped in for a short visit' a few minutes before the shooting occurred, was slightly wounded in the arm. In total, more than forty bullets had been fired into the panic-stricken group.

Five children, who cowered terrified in the next room of the flat, and a number of other adults, including four men who were taken to Bathgate Avenue Station for questioning, escaped the hail of bullets. Questioning the surviving women yielded little information, as they sobbed incoherently. The police indicated that at least two of the occupants of the flat had fled the scene of the crime and that they had even not ruled out the possibility that Coll himself, along with Mike Basile, had been present and had fled on the heels of the departing executioners. This, however, sounds like a bizarre theory, as it is inconceivable that the gunmen would have left without having finished off the main target of their mission.

No weapons were found in the death-house, which was situated two doors away from the house where Bifano had been arrested following Coll's ill-fated, cryptic 'for the boys' message, which the police had construed as a signal that Schultz would soon be sleeping with the fishes.

Comparisons with the St Valentine's Day massacre were inevitable. It was obvious that the killers had known that there would be a meeting of some sort in the apartment that night, possibly to be attended by Coll himself, and had hoped to emulate Al Capone in his massacre of the George 'Bugs' Moran gang in Chicago three years previously. The *Daily News* even suggested that the killers had been especially imported from the Windy City to carry out the task that New York's finest had so far failed to do. The motive for the triple killing was immediately apparent to many, who saw it as an attempt to bag the $50,000 tag that the underworld had placed on Vincent Coll's head. Seen in this light, the St Bridget's Day Massacre (if I may coin a phrase) can be deemed to have been an abject failure. The tabloids dismissed the slaughter as the latest in a long line of bloody incidents in the beer turf battle between Vince and the Dutchman. 'Schultz Mob Kills Two Men and Women in Coll Fort', screamed the leader in the *Daily News*.

Two days later, the abandoned cars that had been used by the murderers were found by the police. Both cars contained small arsenals and had false licence plates that had apparently been smuggled out of Auburn Prison, where they had been manufactured by sympathetic inmates. Despite these leads, the perpetrators of the slaughter were never brought to justice.

The investigating police were confronted with an unusually accommodating informant. Nonchalantly discounting the story that Dutch Schultz had offered a $50,000 reward for his elimination, Vincent Coll offered to tell his old pal Commissioner Mulrooney 'anything he wanted to know'. Not surprisingly, the message, conveyed through the offices of Leibowitz, was declined.

The 4 February edition of the *New York Times* ran with the extraordinary theory that 'members of Coll's gang did the shooting themselves to eliminate "squealers" from their ranks'. The newspaper suggested that information given by some of these people's comrades had helped send Odierno and Giordano to the death-house. Although Coll's outfit was indeed leaky, it is highly unlikely that any members of his crew would have chosen to eliminate their colleagues in front of so many witnesses. Subsequent reporting of the slaughter chose to ignore this theory.

13

HOT DOG

Despite the St Bridget's Day Massacre, the $50,000 tag that had been placed on his head and the announced aim of the police to drive him out of the city, Coll was unwavering in his determination to reach the pinnacle of underworld hierarchy – a clear indication, if any were needed, that he had lost his senses.

His best form of defence was attack: he intended to get his retaliation in first. True to form, however, his bid for supremacy was rash and death-defying rather than enterprising. Hopelessly outnumbered, he was not content with wiping out the Dutchman; he also renewed his war with Madden and the all-powerful Syndicate. His audacity beggars belief. Was he stupid enough to believe that, although his depleted forces had failed to make inroads into the dominion of his Bronx rival, their further depletion would meet with more success – as well as effectively wiping out the entire hierarchy of New York gangdom? Or had his new-found freedom instilled in him a sense of invincibility? But then again, Coll was the sort of gangster for whom rationality was never part of the equation.

Believing Madden to be the least aggressive of the gang

leaders, probably because he still carried a British passport and his continued stay in the United States depended on the whims of the authorities, Coll deduced that he was also the most vulnerable. Being unable to penetrate his stoic veneer, Coll decided that Big Owney was once again the obvious choice to sponsor his feud with Schultz. He invaded the Duke's private fiefdom, the West Side of Manhattan, forcibly impressing upon his speakeasies the need to buy liquor that had been stolen from the Dutchman or his outlets. The net result was that the Syndicate was paying twice or three times over for its own merchandise, as well as being undersold by competitors with its own booze.

By the third week of 1932, things had got so out of hand that an extraordinary general meeting of gangdom was hastily convened in the Forrest Hotel. Every self-respecting gang leader in New York was present, bar one. Vincent Coll had not been asked to attend for the simple reason that he himself was the only item on the agenda. Such had been his impact in the underworld in the three short weeks since his release that it had been deemed necessary to hold a special convention to discuss ways of countering the threat he posed. His wildcat antics threatened to rock the equilibrium of the illicit empires of New York. Those present were confident that the bounty they had placed on his head would eventually reap dividends, but the fear was that it could take months, if not years, for a lone gunman to get close enough to Coll to take a pot-shot at him. None of the gang leaders could run the risk of his prolonged presence in the city, particularly if the level of attrition maintained its current momentum.

It was decided to try another tack. A chink in Coll's armour had been identified. Enrico 'Eddie' Battaglia, a slim, prune-faced youth who had worked intermittently for the Mick, was deemed to be a weak link and to be susceptible to graft. Some reports suggested that he had escaped out of the window of the Cornish Arms with Fats McCarthy just as Vincent Coll and Tuffy Odierno had been arrested. The convention decided that Battaglia should be approached and told in no uncertain terms that he would either put his boss on the spot or face the inevitable consequences.

As well as this, it was agreed at the Forrest Hotel convention that the city would be divided into equal zones, each of which would be manned by gunmen who would eliminate Coll the minute he came into sight. Anxious not to violate the terms of his parole or of the Atlantic City Agreement, Madden imported mercenary assassins from the Midwest – who were not instantly recognisable in Manhattan – to be on hand when such an eventuality arose. Such a stratagem was virtually unheard-of in New York and is a measure of the fear Coll had instilled in his rivals.

But Coll's race was not yet run. He decided to make a full-frontal assault on Madden. The fulcrum and nerve centre of Big Owney's empire was the Phoenix Cereal Beverage Company, a brewery that straddled Tenth Avenue at Twenty-fifth Street. When Prohibition agents had padlocked it years earlier, a tunnel had been drilled under the street to a warehouse, where the illicit beer-brewing continued behind legally locked doors. Though the pungent whiff of hops and malt was the dominant odour of the West Side, much as it is around Guinness's in Dublin, the authorities turned a blind eye – and a blocked nose – to Madden's flagrant flouting of the Eighteenth Amendment. Others were frustrated in their resolute pursuit of justice. One federal agent described to the *Police Gazette* the level of protection the gangster received:

> If you merely parked your car near Twenty-sixth Street
> on Tenth Avenue, where the brewery was located, New
> York policemen would appear from several directions
> and order you to leave 'or else'. Just driving through a
> side street after midnight made the place sound like a
> bird sanctuary. Whistles blew and doors slammed and,
> I suppose, machine-gunners took their stations.

Other gang leaders, like Vannie Higgins and Dutch Schultz,
owed their prosperity to the fact that they operated as
exclusive distributors of Madden's liquor in their respective
spheres of influence. Those operating outside the realms of
this cosy cartel found it impossible to compete, as they had
to haul the booze long distances from New York, Connecticut
or upstate. This added to their overheads, as well as
increasing the risk of interception. The incentive to continue
such an operation was often negated by the risks involved.
The Duke, on the other hand, effectively had police
protection for his activities, and demand for his high-quality
beer, called Madden's Number One, outstripped supply.

Coll underestimated the Duke's astuteness and standing
in the underworld. Violence and extortion were the only
currency Coll could understand. He had also elevated his
'cutting-in' ploy to an obsessive tic. Once again, he presented
Madden with his own brand of Hobson's choice, com-
municating to him that he intended to cut himself in as a
full partner of the Phoenix operation 'or else'. Big Owney
was incensed and refused to dignify the 'request' with an
answer. Coll, who had expected as much, unfurled plan B.

He proposed to kidnap Jack Marron, Madden's brother-in-law, who was a local bail bondsman and a Tammany mandarin. In view of the transparency of his operation to date, Vincent decided to communicate his intentions directly to his quarry. He rang Marron at his offices in a political club at Ninth Avenue and Thirty-fourth Street, demanding that, if Coll did not receive $100,000 cash on delivery, Marron would be taken on a one-way ride in the immediate future. There were to be no cut-rate prices, as there had been in the case of Big Frenchy. These were, after all, inflationary times. Marron had forty-eight hours to decide. Marron was terrified; Coll was not the bluffing type.

Believing a solution to 'the Mick problem' to be imminent, Madden played for time. Instead of issuing a curt refusal, the Duke communicated to Coll that he could not muster up so much cash at such short notice. Before such a deal could be brokered, certain arrangements would have to be ironed out with his associates, many of whom were based in Florida. If, on the other hand, Coll was willing to wait a couple of weeks, Madden believed that things would work out to his rival's satisfaction. Coll granted him a fortnight's stay of execution.

Mad Dog also visited Mike Best, manager of Madden's Cotton Club in Harlem, and demanded money. Best refused, and Coll gave him a week to 'think it over'. Nothing came of his threat, however. Coll also stepped up his attacks on the Syndicate in the wake of the St Bridget's Day massacre, hijacking and destroying beer trucks, seizing booze shipments and bombing beer-drops. A message had been relayed through Marron to the Duke – who was in Florida more for 'health reasons' than as part of any real effort to accommodate

Coll's demands – that 9 February was the final deadline.

Coll had not kept abreast with what was happening in the underworld, however. Rumblings of what was in store for him had obviously reached the ears of Walter Winchell, gossip-meister supreme. Winchell was the most syndicated columnist of his day – his column ran in 2,000 newspapers – and his radio broadcasts were networked throughout the world on Sunday evenings. Born into a poor Jewish neighbourhood in Harlem, 'Mrs Winchell's little boy', as he liked to call himself, caught the rising star of radio and became one of the biggest celebrities of his day. He was an adrenalin junkie whose lure lay in pure, unadulterated gossip. He thrived in a pre-litigation age: his columns were written in glaciated, slangy psychobabble and were by and large scurrilously inaccurate and unscrupulously unverifiable. According to his biographer, Neal Gabler, Winchell viewed gossip as 'a weapon of empowerment for the reader and listener'. He commanded outrageous fees and regarded everybody in the public domain as column-fodder. Only a handful of luminaries avoided being exposed in his column. In later years he made the disturbing political transformation from being a mouthpiece of Franklin D. Roosevelt to being an apologist for red-baiting. As one observer has commented:

> When Winchell broadcast an unbecoming story about an actress, her career was in trouble; when he championed the cause of Joe McCarthy, the country was in trouble.

Winchell always had his finger on the pulse of Prohibition times, frequenting speakeasies such as the Stork Club, where his meals and drinks were always on the house. Though regarded as a character-assassin extraordinare, he could also enhance the reputation of those who curried his favour. He became known as J. Edgar Hoover's 'Man Friday' but also had a hotline to some of the most notorious gangsters of the era. He performed a dangerous juggling act that frequently teetered on disaster.

One day, Winchell went to his barber for a haircut. Sitting in an adjoining chair was Big Owney Madden, and it wasn't long before the two men had struck up a conversation. Ever the egotist, Winchell asked the Duke if the gangster knew who he was, and to his surprise Winchell got an affirmative answer. 'When Madden flattered the jet-propelled columnist by conceding that he had heard of him before, the odd pair got along well,' the *New York Post* later reported. They struck up a friendship – or rather a business relationship. As a British-passport holder who was still on parole, Madden wanted to avoid any undue publicity. It therefore suited him to have New York's main purveyor of dirt on his payroll. Winchell received a $2,000 Stutz Bearcat car and a body-guard for his services, and Madden remained cloaked in anonymity. Thus, in deference to 'the Dook', no mention had been made of Big Frenchy's kidnap. Though Owney drip-fed Winchell with tittle-tattle and idle talk about his rivals, he never fully trusted the columnist either, according to Madden's biographer Graham Nown:

Owney cultivated Winchell but had little respect for him. 'He's anybody's dog,' he would warn friends behind the columnist's back. 'Watch him – he'll hunt with any pack that comes along.' Later, in retirement,

Owney would sit in his lawyer's office in Hot Springs, listening to Winchell's radio broadcasts with his fox terrier on his knee. When a particularly unreliable item tumbled from the wireless among the torrent of 'informed' snippets, Owney would look sceptical. 'I'd check that out,' he would scoff to anyone within earshot.

Disregarding the fact that he was paid by Madden to suppress stories, Winchell could not resist lobbing into one of his columns his tuppence-ha'penny worth about the new faces that had come to town as a result of the Forrest Hotel convention.

If Pegler's article in the *Daily News* a few weeks earlier had been disturbingly prophetic, then a piece that appeared in Winchell's column on 8 February 1932 was positively clairvoyant. In his 'On Broadway' column in the bulldog edition of that day's *Daily Mirror*, the gossip columnist wrote a typically irresponsible piece that would shortly have far-reaching consequences for himself:

Five planes brought dozens of machine gats from Chicago Friday to combat The Town's Capone . . . Local banditti have made one hotel a virtual arsenal and several hot spots are ditto because Master Coll is giving them the headache . . . One of the better Robin Hoods has a phone in his cell! . . . Haw!

The paper hit the street a few hours before Master Coll made his last phone call.

14

DOG PUT DOWN

As a result of Mulrooney's tactics of harrassment and the underworld bounty that had been placed on Coll's head, Vincent and Lottie had been constantly on the move since the gangster's release from custody. Curiously, they had chosen to hole up in the Cornish Arms Hotel, a place that was clearly associated with them. With the benefit of hindsight, this seems like an odd decision in view of the fact that they had both been arrested there a couple of months previously, amid extensive media coverage, and that the hotel was situated barely a block and a half away from Owney Madden's penthouse apartment.

On the evening of 8 February, Vincent drove to the Irish stronghold of Sunnyside, New Jersey, to meet up with some local hoods about a possible snatch. He was accompanied by one of his bodyguards. Fearing that he would be picked up once again by the police, he could not afford to carry firearms. The conclave was completed by about eleven o'clock, and it was past midnight by the time the two men rolled off the ferry at Twenty-third Street. The moon was like a scooped-out melon as Coll made his way home in the quavery, grey dawn. Whether he got a glimpse at the early edition of the *Daily Mirror* is something we will never know, but it would appear that his suspicions had not been aroused.

The two men did not go directly home that night; instead, they strolled into the London Chemists drugstore at 314 West Twenty-third Street, which had a late opening. The store, which was directly across the road from the Cornish Arms, still exists, though its premises have moved about fifty metres up the road. There were five others in the drugstore when Coll and his bodyguard entered, at about 1.10 am. Dr Leo Katz, who was on holiday from Chicago, was standing at the soda fountain sipping an orangeade. Jean Scott, the prescription clerk, was serving the neighbourhood physician, Dr Edward Pravaner, under the watchful eye of her superior, Morris Kernowitz. Also present was Peggy Bonner, who would have come into contact with Coll through her work at the Cornish Arms Hotel. The proprietor, Jacob Harris, stood outside, conversing with a customer.

Coll had some unfinished business to attend to. The stay of execution he had granted Madden had elapsed, and his patience was running out. He entered a phone booth at the rear of the shop and rang Madden to demand his loot. He probably did not get through to Big Owney, however, as the Duke had conveniently gone to Florida for 'health reasons'. Whoever he spoke to kept him on the line for as long as possible. His bodyguard, meanwhile, had treacherously told his boss that he had to ring his moll. He went into the adjacent telephone booth and made a short but highly significant call. Then he sat by the soda fountain.

After Coll had been in the booth for ten minutes or so, a limousine pulled up. The driver alighted, holding a machine-gun which was partly obscured by his greatcoat, and covered the door. Two other men walked forward. Of these, one stopped in the doorway, and the other, machine-gun in clear view, marched towards the booth. He winked at Coll's bodyguard and jerked his thumb in a signal for him to leave. The bodyguard slid quietly out of the door.

'All right, everybody,' the gunman said calmly, 'keep cool and you won't get hurt.'

The clerks ducked under the counter, and Dr Katz sat motionless where he was. The gunman then took three paces forward until he was in direct line with the telephone booth. Vincent, still talking into the phone, with his lips pressed close to the mouthpiece, was completely unaware of what was going on behind him.

Coll was almost cleaved in half as the sputtering tommy-gun pumped him full of lead. Fifteen .45-calibre, steel-jacketed slugs were fired, and all fifteen found their mark.

As the killer backed out of the store, the door of the booth opened slowly and Coll's perforated body pitched forward, three bullets in the head, three in the chest, one in the abdomen and eight in the arms and legs. The blunt bleat of the disengaged telephone cut through the sequinned gloom.

His task completed, the gunman turned and, giving the signal to his companions, ran swiftly from the store. The three tossed their 'choppers' into the rear of the limo that was parked on the kerb outside the drugstore, climbed in and sped into the lambent morning.

While out on his beat, Patrolman James Sherlock had heard the withering report of the automatics. In a scene reminiscent of *The Untouchables,* he jumped on the running-board of a cab and gave chase, firing at the killers as they hurtled out of Twenty-third Street into Eighth Avenue. Though Sherlock rode the running-board all the way to Fiftieth Street, the limousine, travelling at an estimated 70 mph, soon outdistanced the cab.

Meanwhile, Detective Francis C. Trainor, who lived in the Cornish Arms, was alerted by Peggy Bonner. He rushed to the drugstore, only to find that Lottie, still dressed in her blue-polka-dot 'wedding' attire, had beaten him to the scene. She sobbed hysterically, falling to her knees and screaming, 'That's my Vincent! Let me back! The dirty rats – oh, the dirty rats!'

How the news of her husband's slaying was relayed to Lottie so quickly remains a mystery. The media later made hay from the fact that, although she was still in her early twenties, she had now been widowed three times.

Coll was formally pronounced dead by Dr John Bullard, an ambulance surgeon from New York Hospital. According to the autopsy, the bullet holes extended from the bottom of the right arm in a zigzagging line to the top of the victim's head. Two slugs entered the right side of the head at the back of the ear; one pierced the right shoulder, while the other shattered the right side of the face. A further four bullets went through the left forearm, and seven entered the right arm between the elbow and the shoulder. Four of the latter shots perforated the body, but three passed into the right side of the chest and lodged there. Five slugs that had passed through the corpse lodged in Coll's clothing, while the rest became embedded in the back wall of the phone booth. Coll's death certificate lists 'bullet wounds of head and brain, right chest, right lung and heart' as the cause of death. Within hours, newsboys hawked an extra edition, with the cry of 'Baby-killer slain! They got the baby-killer!'

A crowd of more than two dozen people congregated outside the store as the young gangster's body was removed to the morgue. A shock of golden curls was all that was visible above the blanket as police stretchered his torn torso from the drugstore. Florence later had the body removed to the Walter Cooke Funeral Parlour, at 142 Street and Willis Avenue, the Bronx, where, in accordance with the custom of the day, it remained on view for two days. There was apparently no shortage of curious onlookers congregating outside the parlour, anxious to get a glimpse of Coll's corpse. Police on duty there denied admission, though. When informed that Florence had claimed the body and was arranging to give him a Christian burial, Lottie reacted angrily. 'That isn't nice,' she rasped. 'Mrs Reddan probably doesn't know what she is saying or doing.'

As Coll's body was removed from the store, the police held Lottie for questioning. She had many questions to answer, particularly concerning how she had arrived so quickly at the scene of the crime. Cold and defiant, the only explanation she offered was that 'some man called me at my home in the Bronx and said that Vincent was hurt'. This was a rather cryptic explanation, for although the couple always gave their address as 1465 Jessup Avenue, the Bronx, they had in reality been holed up in the Cornish Arms for some time. Detectives informed her that Coll's bodyguard had walked from the store without so much as a murmur of protest when the assassins appeared. She professed ignorance of the fact that the young gangster had ever had a bodyguard and made no reply to suggestions that this man was the one who had telephoned her. 'I don't want to appear stubborn,' she said, 'but I don't know anything. And if I did know anything, I wouldn't tell you.' Convinced that further questioning was a waste of time and that she had no intention of helping the forces of justice avenge the death of the man she professed to love, Police Commissioner Mulrooney ordered her release.

Later in the day, Lottie appeared at Leibowitz's offices in Brooklyn, where she gave an impromptu press conference. Despite some sassy soundbites, she said nothing that might conceivably have put her head on the block.

She was wearing a shabby brown dress and a cheap outfit – very different from the conventional attire of a gangster's moll. It was as if she had employed a handler in her moment of grief to maximise the effect of what she had to say. She told the press that all her clothing, including a couple of expensive fur coats, had disappeared at the time the state troopers had raided her and Coll's Albany hideout.

To her vague answers on the subject of the telephone notification of Coll's death, she added that, 'The person who phoned got the information from another party. He just relayed the message.' She did not elaborate, however, as to how, or by whom, the message was passed on in such a short time. According to her story, she had maintained a terror-stricken vigil when Coll had failed to return for his dinner. The vigil had eventually been broken by the mystery phone call early that Monday morning; she had been told to get her hat and come and look at her dead husband.

Lottie said that she did not know any of Coll's business and denied having had any part in his depredations. She told journalists that the couple, far from plotting to annex the underworld supremacy of Madden or Schultz, had been planning 'a nice honeymoon trip to Ireland'. In view of his insolvency, however, she amended her statement by saying, 'That is, we were going if Vincent could get hold of any money.'

The thought of Vincent and Lottie disembarking at Derry, boarding the Lough Swilly train to Mín Doire Dhamh and cutting a swagger in Bunbeg with their fur coats and custom-fitted suits and all the attendant airs and graces beggars belief. Would Coll have been treated as a pariah who had brought shame to his home parish or, as was the case in Sicily, might he have been fêted as a hero – the local boy made bad.

The report of the killing in the morning edition of the *Daily News* threw in some unverifiable innuendo about a possible adulterous affair involving Coll. 'Perhaps it was sentiment that took him there,' the paper speculated. 'Perhaps, like Jack Diamond, he had a particularly significant reason for straying from his hearth – someone in the vicinity of West Twenty-third Street, another Kiki.'

Such a suggestion does not merit serious consideration, however. Though it would make a great story, there is no evidence to suggest that Coll had a secret paramour or that his jealous partner had hired assassins to avenge his adulterous behaviour. Nor are there any grounds for believing that Lottie had her 'husband' put on the spot in order to gain possession of his wealth. Coll had squandered the massive revenue generated by his kidnapping exploits and had died a pauper. The sum of $101 was found marinated in gore in the pocket of his suit, while a further $100 was unearthed in his hotel room. Beyond that, he left no estate.

The absence of a murder motive notwithstanding, it

remains a mystery as to how Lottie arrived on the scene of the slaying so rapidly. Most of the speculation about any possible involvement by her in the crime, however, hinged on the fact that her previous two husbands had met with a similar fate.

15

A Dog's End

Even in death, Vincent Coll courted controversy. He was buried without bell, book or candle. At the last minute, the church, in keeping with its usual policy towards gangsters, interdicted any funeral rites. A church service announced by Florence had to be hastily cancelled. The church did allow Coll's body to be buried in hallowed ground, however, as the gangster had apparently made Confession shortly before his death. Nonetheless, no priest was allowed to officiate at the interment.

Only one message of condolence arrived for Lottie. It came from Alice Diamond, the widow of Legs, who had been killed a few weeks earlier. 'Please accept my sincere sympathy,' wired Mrs Diamond, who was touring the vaudeville theatres at the time with a one-act tell-all sketch about her life with the deceased gangster.

On the brittle winter morning of 11 February, Vincent Coll was buried in St Raymond's Cemetery in the Bronx. There was none of the usual gangland pomp surrounding his obsequies. None of the underworld's 'big shots', who were all still busily breathing sighs of relief, could be bothered going through the usual motions of paying their last respects.

There was no need for any such pretence on this occasion.

A knot of curious bystanders turned up at the Walter B. Cooke funeral parlour in the Bronx to see the gangster being brought out. Coll's riddled body was in an imitation-metallic coffin. Neither Lottie nor Florence apparently had the financial wherewithal to provide him with a more expensive coffin or to arrange the usual showy gangster funeral. On top of his coffin was a blanket of red and white flowers. Woven into the centre in white blooms was the legend 'From the Boys'. Two cars of mourners followed the hearse, with Lottie, Florence, Joe and Frank Reddan in the first one. Two open cars filled with flowers followed, and the cortège was completed by four carloads of detectives.

St Raymond's Cemetery was sheathed in a dense, spectral fog as the professional pall-bearers carried the coffin over a muddy lane to the open grave where Vincent's brother Peter had been buried nine months previously. A dozen or so mourners picked their way behind the procession. Lottie was inconsolable and wept continuously. In the mud and chill, the little group gathered around the grave. It was a far cry from the lavish gangster funerals of Chicago or the no-expense-spared ceremony that Dutch Schultz had laid on for his loyal stooge Dangerous Dan Iamascia in the same plot several months previously. Iamascia, it will be recalled, was one of the first to perish during the Coll-Schultz feud and was rewarded for his faithfulness with a $10,000 coffin. No such pomp was to be afforded for those who broke away.

As the rain died into a quiescent drizzle, the undertaker's assistant recited the Our Father and Hail Mary in a hurried monotone. A bevy of reporters and detectives stood in the silence, and the gravediggers, blurred and indistinct in the background, leaned on their implements. At the head of the grave was the massive granite headstone that Vincent had erected for Peter, on which the words 'In loving memory of my brother' were inscribed. The casket sank slowly into the grave. Lottie sobbed. Vincent Coll was buried. The handful of mourners scattered like chaff, with the detectives in close attendance, hoping in vain for a break that would furnish them with a new lead in their investigation of the Coll killing.

Ironically, one of the few tributes paid to the dead man came from an unlikely source. Speaking to Joseph Driscoll, of the *Herald Tribune,* Police Commissioner Mulrooney described Coll as 'a real tough fellow'. 'He was no Diamond. If he wanted a job done, he would go and do it himself,' he said. Despite this qualified eulogy, the general feeling in New York was that the city was a better place without Coll.

*

So who did kill Mad Dog Coll? The possibilities are legion. He had ruffled the feathers of some important people during his meteoric rise to notoriety, and this complicated the search for his murderers. There appeared to be a waiting list to kill Coll. It was no secret that Schultz, Madden, Luciano and Terranova were all gunning for him. What was unclear was which of them had got to him first. The smart money says that it was the Dutchman, possibly working in collusion with Madden. Popular perception has it that Bo Weinberg, Schultz's top assassin, whom Coll had shamed in the Brook Avenue speakeasy a couple of years previously, had exacted his vengeance. The author E. L. Doctorow has him admit as much in his fine novel *Billy Bathgate*:

He was a greaser of consequence, Maranzano, not some piece of crazed slime like Coll who you couldn't ever put enough bullets in. Not like Coll, that mick fuck of a child-killer, for whom one death was not enough. But I killed Coll! he shouted. I turned him to spit and shit and blood in that phone booth. Brrrrupp! Up one window. Brrrrupp! Down the other. I killed him!

In his memoirs, Dixie Davies, the Dutchman's lawyer, suggests that, while Bo had indeed taken part in the incident, he had stood aside in favour of an even surer marksman. Davies maintains that Weinberg was in fact the driver that day. Such was the importance of the occasion that many argue that the services of the super-assassin Red Levine, an Orthodox Jew who would not kill on the Sabbath, had been enlisted.

It has also been suggested that the assassin was Coll's former comrade-in-arms Fats McCarthy. On the night of his murder, Coll had somehow given two undercover cops who had been trailing him for a number of weeks the slip. A round-the-clock tail had been placed on Vincent in the hope that he might lead them to his pike-lipped partner, who was sought in connection with the killing of Detective Guido Passagno the previous October, not to mention that of Legs Diamond just before Christmas. Fats McCarthy was effectively a freelance gun for hire; he was not shackled by either membership of any one gang or undue regard for sentimentality or friendship. The police had no evidence that any serious fissures had emerged in their alliance or that there had been any formal parting of the ways. It is entirely feasible, though, that Fats would accept the Coll contract from his former boss, Dutch Schultz, particularly if there had been any discrepancy in the sharing-out of spoils. It would have been high irony indeed if Coll, who had for once slipped the police net, had been mown down by the very man the police had hoped he would lead them to.

The following July, McCarthy was trailed to a hideaway outside Albany with his wife and two others and perished in the ensuing shootout. Detective Harold Moore was shot three times in the incident before he eventually put a bullet in McCarthy's head.

Mike Basile was captured in the same shoot-out and sentenced to seventeen to thirty-five years in Dannemora Prison – the Siberia of New York. Still smarting over his brother's execution on St Bridget's Day, Basile largely fits the description of the double-crossing bodyguard. Owney Madden's forces had already sussed out Enrico Battaglia, whom they identified as a weak link in the Coll chain, and he may indeed have been the man who stepped aside so readily when the gunmen entered the store.

Another possible traitor was Joe Marino, a recent defector from the Dutchman's operation and a man with whom Coll had been spending a great deal of time in the past number of weeks. Was his desertion from the Schultz ranks genuine or had he in fact been placed in situ, on standby for a suitable occasion for betrayal?

The day after the murder, Commissioner Mulrooney said that the police had nothing to link the death with any of the head honchos of gangland. He declared the killing to be 'a positive defiance of law and order' – a slight understatement, in the circumstances. 'I hear Madden and De Mange are in

Florida,' he said, 'and the others are all where we can reach them, if we want to pick them up. I think it's true that the $100 is all the money he had. We didn't find any traces of all these "grands" that are talked about. The city is well rid of him. Of course we will try to solve the case. This is a government of laws not of men, as I believe Mayor Gaynor once said.'

Assistant District Attorney George Carney of the Homicide Bureau was assigned to investigate the case. Unlike the Harlem baby-killing, there was no clamour for justice or pressure to come up with instant results. If truth be told, the American people regarded the perpetrators as stout-hearted heroes who had performed a public service. Carney had very little to go on. The accounts of the five eyewitnesses did not quite tally and offered scant details. It was established, however, that the licence plates on the limo had been part of the shipment stolen from Auburn Prison, where they had been manufactured by inmates. These plates tallied with some from the same shipment that had been found on the vehicles abandoned after the massacre in the Bronx. A subsequent investigation of the shipment yielded nothing, however.

Many stories were circulating that Coll's killers had been sleepers imported from Kansas City, Chicago, Detroit, St Louis or even Los Angeles. Others fingered Leonard Scarnici as the triggerman. On 29 May 1933, Scarnici was apprehended in Troy after an abortive bank heist that had resulted in the death of a detective. When the bullets from the gun used in that incident were compared to those in Coll's it was clear that they did not match. Although Scarnici admitted to leading the Schultz offensive on Coll's lair in

Commonwealth Avenue on St Bridget's Day 1932, reporters continued to attribute Coll's murder to him as well, right up to the point when he was executed in the electric chair on 27 June 1935.

On 19 September 1939, Big Frenchy De Mange passed away peacefully in his sleep in the Hotel Warwick. At the funeral, many were startled to see a young stranger who bore an uncanny resemblence to Coll. One of De Mange's entourage tipped off a crime reporter that this young man was in fact the assassin that had been imported from Detroit to kill the Mick. It would have been an odd twist of fate indeed if, in a complete reversal of the Sloane incident of May 1931, Coll had been put on the spot by a veritable clone.

Perhaps the most outlandish theory was the one in which Harry Behan, an inmate of Great Meadows Penitentiary, was supposed to have been spirited away from detention for one night to settle an old score with Coll. Behan was serving a long sentence at the time for robbing jewellery belonging to the wife of the playwright Howard Johnson. According to this bizarre theory, the Syndicate had secured his release for one night to perform the execution before slipping him back into prison. Having the perfect alibi, Behan was of course above suspicion.

In the absence of any concrete evidence, all eyes turned to Winchell, whose prophetic piece in the *Daily Mirror* had forecast Coll's death mere hours before it had occurred. What had he meant when he referred to five airplanes, loaded with gunmen, having been sent from Chicago to end the racketeering activities of Master Coll? Furthermore, who had furnished him with his information?

Winchell's nervousness about a Madden backlash was apparent when his next article appeared, a week to the day after Coll's murder. 'If only, when my epitaph is readied, they will say: Here is Walter Winchell with his ear to the ground – as usual,' he wrote.

In another article he also hinted that things were getting a bit hot for him in New York: 'If I had the moxie I would chuck the whole thing and go somewhere with her [his wife] and the children and laugh a little.'

Before he could properly entertain such a suggestion, Mrs Winchell's little boy was subpoenaed by Assistant District Attorney Carney to appear before the grand jury investigating Coll's death on 17 February 1932.

For thirty minutes, Winchell defied his natural instincts and held his wheest as he testified on the manner in which he had obtained his information. He refused to divulge his sources to the grand jurors. On advice from his lawyer, he had also refused to make any statement to Carney before taking the witness stand.

The story he told the grand jury was a simple one. A waiter in a speakeasy had slipped him a note, which he had immediately destroyed. Conveniently enough, he could recall neither the speakeasy nor what the waiter looked like. (It was later revealed, however, that he had been given the tip-off by Texas Guinan, a brassy night-club hostess and a valuable font of good gossip.) When asked if it was his policy to publish anonymous tip-offs without checking their veracity, he said simply 'yes'. After all, asking a gangster to confirm or deny whether he intended to kill a rival would be an exercise in futility. While delivering his testimony, Winchell appeared jittery and tense, but his fears were soon dispelled when some of the jurors enquired about getting passes to Broadway plays. The grand jury had accepted Winchell's woolly explanation.

As he left the courtroom he was gruff with fellow hacks, using the fact that he was legally prohibited from disclosing information on the proceedings and his apparent lack of sleep for the previous twenty-nine hours as an excuse for his rudeness. As he brushed past the scrum of photographers, his only comment was, 'I'm no heel; I'll stand up to be shot.' He later admitted to Stanley Walker, the veteran editor of the *Daily News*, 'I lost seven more pounds, I think, testifying before the grand jury that time.'

Winchell's prediction of Coll's demise had sent shock waves through the underworld. He had gone a little too close to the bone on this occasion, particularly in light of the fact that Madden was currently embroiled in a legal wrangle, with efforts being made by the authorities to have him returned to Sing Sing for parole violations. The day after Coll had been shot, Winchell received phone threats at the NBC studios and at his hotel suite telling him in no uncertain terms that he would be taken for a ride if he did not desist from printing stories about New York gangsters. Paul Sweinhart reported in the entertainment trade paper *Zits Weekly*, for example, that 'a certain daily newspaper columnist will be bumped off in six months.' On top of this, a Philadelphia journalist declared, 'We hereby notify Walter Winchell that he's likely to be shot any day now.'

This prompted Winchell to show up at Forty-seventh Street Police Station, where he asked for − and received − twenty-four-hour police protection. He was described by officers on duty as 'nervous and in genuine fear of his life.'

According to *Time* magazine, rumours were circulating that Winchell had placed the names of would-be assassins in a secure deposit box. This prompted the gossip-monger to joke to his friend Robert Benchley of the *New Yorker*, 'Dear Bob, see you at the New Yorker Theater tonight. Don't worry about anything as I have just been killed.' Despite his bravado it was obvious that Winchell was feeling the heat.

Shortly afterwards, the *Daily Mirror* announced that the column was to be discontinued until further notice because Winchell had taken an extended family holiday in California, having apparently suffered a nervous breakdown. Six weeks later, he eased himself back into work. 'By then the party, or parties, most seriously distressed by his extraordinary foresight in the Coll murder, [had] cooled off,' reported the *New York Post*. It was later claimed that Owney had spared him his life only after he had received a payment of $90,000 by way of extortion.

Though it healed the wounds, the passage of time could not exorcise Winchell's memory of the distress he had experienced at the time, as he later recalled in an interview:

> I turned green. I was sick to my stomach. I learned later that Coll had a list of names in his pocket when he was shot – names of people he intended to murder. Mine was on it.

It was a number of years before he attempted to tackle a serious gangland exposé again. Winchell's reputation amongst the mob was eventually rehabilitated, however, on 24 August 1940, when the infamous Louis Lepke, head of Murder Inc, used him as a go-between to hand himself over to the authorities after more than two years on the lam.

By an odd quirk of fate, Winchell was later employed as the hyperactive announcer of *The Untouchables,* in which both Coll and Madden featured prominently. The series debuted in 1959 and lasted four seasons. Ironically, it was produced by Lucille Ball's production company Desilu. Ball herself had taken great exception, a few years previously, to being wrongly outed by Winchell as a red during Senator McCarthy's communist witch-hunt.

Carney's investigation spluttered on for several months without ever gaining much momentum. Wild speculation, coupled with the underworld wall of silence, made a breakthrough virtually impossible. Though many theories had been widely touted, there was no substantive supportive evidence for any of them. The case ended up gathering dust on the shelves of the homicide squad alongside the numerous other 'open' cases for which Mad Dog himself had been responsible.

16

GONE TO THE DOGS

After Coll had been slain, Lottie received no benefits from her husband's estate. He had effectively died penniless, with a mere hundred dollars in his jacket pocket. This left Lottie high and dry. She was not at liberty to relaunch her criminal career, though. When detectives had arrested Coll at the Cornish Arms Hotel the previous October, a loaded pistol had been found in her possession. On 26 February 1932, a fortnight after her husband's murder, she was found guilty of the charge in Special Sessions Court. Whether they wanted to monitor her movements in light of the outstanding questions that needed to be answered or whether they genuinely feared for her life or her health – she seemed to have become addicted to sedatives – the police requested that she be admitted as a patient to the Fordham Hospital pending her arraignment for sentence. There she remained, under police guard, for almost three months; then, on 18 June, Justice Herbert in the Court of Special Sessions sentenced her to serve six months in the workhouse. The sentence was to include the period spent in Fordham, which meant that Mrs Coll, as she was now referred to, served a term of less than two months, most of which she spent in the workhouse hospital.

On her release from detention, she was plunged into a maelstrom of uncertainty and consequently faded briefly into obscurity. She had a lavish lifestyle to maintain, however, and in the absence of another impressionable young gangster she would have to fend for herself. Her next foray into the world of crime would lead to tragedy, though.

*

At the stroke of eleven on the night of 21 June 1933, the muffled squawks of a radio dispatch jarred police officers James Kohler and Edward Gallagher from the monotony of their north Bronx beat. 'Cars 172, 173, 174, investigate shooting near 1175 Wheeler Avenue. Signal thirty,' droned the announcer. Signal thirty indicated that a violent crime had occurred. By the time their little green roadster had screeched to a halt at the address, a small crowd had assembled in the sleepy middle-class residential street. The air was humid with blood. Lying limp on the sidewalk was the body of a young girl. Her distraught father identified the girl as seventeen-year-old Millie Schwartz. From his preliminary examination, Assistant Medical Examiner Dr Louis Lefkkowitz concluded that a bullet had entered her cheek, torn through the muscles of her throat and cracked two of the vertebrae in her spine. In addition, her spinal cord had been severed. He presented the two officers with the offending bullet – a .38 calibre.

Her near-hysterical sister informed them of the circum-stances of the wanton, merciless killing. 'We had been talking under the canopy here, when I heard several shots fired,' she told the officers. 'I saw a car parked up the street and something told me there was danger. I started to run. "Millie, come on!" I said to my sister, and I held out my hand for her to run with me. Thinking that she was following me, I ran for the nearest doorway. When I got inside, she was not there so I turned around and went into the street. I saw her body lying on the sidewalk, running with blood. That is the last I can remember. I know I screamed for help.' (from *True Detective*, May 1935)

The police were faced with a welter of conflicting rumours and counter-rumours including the possibility that Millie Schwartz had been involved in some kind of illicit love affair. All such rumours proved to be unfounded. The accounts of two of the eyewitnesses seemed more credible, however. Hilding Erickson, who had been a valet to James J. Walker, a former mayor of New York and one-time great white hope of Irish America, and Andrew Jorgenson, a retired real-estate agent, reported seeing a gunfight between two young men – one in a sedan and the other on the sidewalk. It would appear that Millie Schwartz was unfortunate enough to be caught in the crossfire. Regrettably, neither Erickson nor Jorgenson was able to identify the assailants when presented with a wide range of photofits in the Bureau of Criminal Identification the following day. In addition, nobody had reported an attempted assault, and the police investigation was left with no clue as to the motive for the killing.

On 23 June, however, the investigating detectives were confronted with a seemingly unconnected piece of intelligence. Word had reached Police Headquarters from 'confidential sources' that Lottie Coll was registered at a midtown hotel. The police had been on her trail for a week because a score of robbery victims had tentatively identified her as the blonde-haired bandit who had terrorised them with the aid of two accomplices. Detectives Roger J. Meehan and Neil Winberry were assigned to the case. The manager of a big hotel in West Forty-third Street, in the heart of the theatrical district, identified Lottie as the occupant of Room 603 and issued the detectives with a pass-key. The two men crept stealthily into the suite, where they were confronted with a strange scene. There before them in the room's twin beds were two men and a woman, all fast asleep and oblivious to the intrusion. The police identified the occupant of the first bed as Joseph Ventre, a spud-faced man in his early thirties with a tangled mass of hair. A swarthy spiv named Alfred Guarino lay in the other bed, asleep in the arms of Lottie Coll – who was not blonde, as had been expected, but dark.

While Meehan covered the sleeping figures, Winberry reached softly under the pillows in search of hidden weapons. He found nothing. A search of the wardrobe proved equally fruitless, as the three occupants remained motionless amidst all the creaking and stirring. Winberry's attention then turned to a cheap leather suitcase in the corner of the room; in the case he found a cache of three unloaded revolvers. Having located the arsenal, Meehan indicated to his partner that it was time to wake the slumberers. Meehan lashed out at Ventre's bed; Ventre in turn writhed uneasily before sitting bolt upright in a stupor. The flash of a shield greeted Guarino as he was shocked into consciousness, while Lottie clutched wildly at a bed-sheet and pulled it up to her chin, covering her abbreviated lingerie.

'What the hell do you want?' she rasped, as she gingerly wiped the film of sleep from her eyes.

'Take it easy, Lottie,' Winberry countered, 'and tell your boyfriend to get out of bed. You're all under arrest.'

Guarino was ordered to get dressed, followed by Ventre.

'Can I get fixed up now?' Lottie pleaded, her bare legs dangling over the side of the bed.

'Go ahead,' said Meehan, according to an account in *True Detective*. 'But no tricks. You can take your clothes into the bathroom and dress there.'

Lottie ambled over to the wardrobe with the sheet draped over her shoulders. She retrieved a blue and white polka-dot dress and a pair of alligator shoes. On her way to the bathroom, she stopped at the dressing table, looked in the mirror and started to pat her tousled hair into some sort of presentable state.

'I just want to powder my nose,' she implored, as she stealthily opened the top drawer.

Meehan was at her side in a flash, gripping her hand. She drew back the hand, wincing with pain.

In the drawer was a lady's handbag weighed down by a loaded .32-calibre revolver.

Meehan thrust her towards the bathroom and ordered her to get dressed promptly.

Unperturbed, Lottie broke into a flashing smile as broad as a gate. 'All right, big shot,' she was reported to have said, contemptuously.

While she was dressing, Meehan rang for assistance. It was a fraught situation, laden with menace. The two detectives were outnumbered, and both Ventre and Guarino refused to put their hands in the air. The constant to-ing and fro-ing added to the unease. Meehan searched the room comprehensively but only unearthed fragments of jewellery and the minute sum of eleven dollars five cents.

Reinforcements arrived presently, and the three suspects were carted off to the West Forty-seventh Street Police Station, where they were booked on charges of robbery. Victims of the gang were brought in and six New York shopkeepers fingered Lottie as the person who had instigated the robberies, calmly directing operations as Ventre and Guarino did the spadework.

'Those are the fellows,' one drugstore clerk was reported to have said, 'and that's the woman who said, "Get those hands up, you mug!"' The fact that she was no longer blonde led the police to conclude that she must have been wearing a wig while the hold-ups took place.

Lottie regarded her victims with dispassionate scorn and cursed with no real spleen. 'You have pretty good memories, boys, but you're all wrong,' she sneered.

Once the watch-chains, tie clips and odds and ends of jewellery that had been found in her room were positively identified by a victim of a hold-up at 184 Willis Avenue, however, Lottie knew she was in trouble.

She was whisked away to police headquarters, where she was paraded on a big stage in a huge auditorium and given a vigorous interrogation by several dozen top-ranking police officers. The thought must have crossed their minds that here was a woman who could easily have graced another catwalk had she not chosen a more disreputable path. White-faced but nonchalant, Lottie cut a dash under the Klieg lights in her blue polka-dot dress, white hat and dark shoes, exchanging repartee with her interrogators. A tiger posing as a pussy cat, she parried a drumbeat of questions from Acting Inspector James E. McGrath with composure and disdain. This was Lottie at her most hard-boiled – an unflappable force of nature, portraying herself as a wronged woman.

'Where do you live?' was McGrath's opening gambit.

'Never mind that,' snarled the champion of deceit and cunning. 'I live with respectable people. I don't want them brought into this.'

'Well, you were staying at a hotel with two men, weren't you?'

'What of it?'

'You know one of them had a bad record?'

'I don't know anything about their records,' came the muffled reply.

'But you lived with one of them at the hotel. Which one was your sweetheart?'

'Neither. They are just my friends. My sweetheart is dead,' she retorted, tapping impatiently with one foot.

'Who killed him,' prodded McGrath. 'Why don't you get that off your chest now?'

Lottie's winced as her voice quietened to a whisper. 'I don't know,' she admitted, in a tone of sad resignation. 'I wish I did.'

She admitted ownership of the foreign-made pistol found in her handbag at the time of her arrest but denied any knowledge of three other weapons which were found in a suitcase that belonged to one of her two companions.

She was interrogated further back in the Eighteenth Precinct, as the police tried to piece together the movements of the gang over the previous few months. She was held in the squad room while her two companions were given the third degree in an adjoining room. The incessant grilling began to take its toll on Lottie, who was becoming increasingly restless and irritable. Her jittery behaviour did not go unnoticed by Winberry and Meehan, who were filling out confidential reports on the case. Meehan decided to seize the opportunity to put the wind up Coll's widow. He framed his interrogation as a series of suggestions.

'Say,' he ventured, in a low, conspiratorial tone, 'do you remember how Vincent was picked up on a gun charge after the ballistics bureau had made an identification?'

Lottie's ears pricked up at the mention of her dead partner and her gaze flickered up to her interrogator. Meehan had cleverly gauged that her love for the dead gangster was like a faulty mechanism that could not be repaired. He had roused a dormant echo of an old passion.

'Well, one of those guns we picked up in your room is hot,' Meehan continued. This was completely untrue; it was a manoeuvre intended to weaken Lottie's steely attitude.

'Which one?' she asked, as she swayed uneasily on her feet.

'The big one,' came the reply.

'What job?' she inquired, with feigned insouciance, but Meehan refused to elaborate as he shrewdly gauged the impact of his words. Lottie's signals of unease were seen as confirmation that she was involved in more serious crimes than the robberies, and she was consequently held for questioning that night. She was charged in West Side Court on two charges of violating the Sullivan Law, and she tittered giddily at Magistrate Walsh as she was led away to Jefferson Market Prison. The news of her arrest was leaked to the press, and late editions carried the story of the detention of the late gangster's moll. As a result of this unwanted publicity, the police received information that was instrumental in the eventual cracking of the case. At ten o'clock that night, an anonymous caller demanded to speak to the officer in charge of detectives. He identified himself as Isadore 'Izzy' Moroh and informed the captain that he would meet one of his detectives in the Bedford Cafeteria the following morning in order to impart some information relating to one of their investigations. Moroh had received a suspended sentence some years previously for grand larceny when he admitted to having purchased stolen dresses. Detective William Colby, who was more than familiar with Moroh's pedigree, arrived at the rendezvous the next morning.

His old client was there before him and greeted him with the news that he had information about the man who had run away from a stick-up a couple of nights before. He confessed to being that man.

'Why didn't you tell us this before?' demanded Colby.

'Huh?' said Moroh, with a wolfish grin. 'Am I crazy? The papers said the police were figuring that the man running away was the gunman. When the story came out that you fellows changed your mind about that, I decided to talk.'

'Who did the job?'

'Three birds that the coppers picked up yesterday - Lottie Coll and her pals.'

Colby ferried Moroh to police headquarters, where he started spilling the beans. Moroh, it transpired, had been operating a money-lending scam from a premises between Elder and Westchester Avenues, where the transactions of his loan business took place. He bumped into Joseph Ventre, an old acquaintance, on the evening of 11 June. On hearing that Ventre was down on his luck and shacked up in a garage, Moroh handed him a dollar to buy some food. A short while later, Ventre returned with some jewellery, which he offered to offload at a competitive rate. Moroh declined the offer but was persuaded to loan Ventre five dollars for a week. Chief Assistant District Attorney Sylvester Ryan later described what happened when Moroh and Ventre met up again on 21 June.

'A friend of mine wants some information on the "EL",' Ventre implored, referring to the Elmira Reformatory, the correctional institution that had served as a finishing school for Coll. He told him that his friend was waiting down the block by Wheeler Avenue. The still street was gripped by a deathly silence, which was punctuated only by the shards of laughter that came from a group of girls who were standing outside one of the apartments. They drew up to a car in the middle of the block.

'Izzy,' said Ventre, when they reached the car, 'I want you to meet Lottie.'

'Where's your friend?' asked Moroh.

'He'll be right back,' said Ventre.

Lottie motioned him into the car, but when he refused she stopped beating around the bush. She offered to sell him a two-and-a-half-carat diamond ring.

'You never saw a ring that size,' he reportedly mocked.

Lottie flashed an anodyne smile. 'You are very foolish not to buy that ring,' she hissed.

The whole situation had a sinister air about it, and Moroh was overcome by a pervading sense of menace. He began to get the heebie-jeebies. He adopted a poker face as a defence mechanism, and when Ventre playfully asked him for change of a $1,000 bill, he reached into his pocket and extracted a thick wad of notes that amounted to the princely sum of $923.

'Now,' said Moroh, 'Where's your friend?'

'He'll be here any minute,' Ventre replied, reassuringly.

Through the lengthening shadows of the evening, Moroh caught sight of a figure lurking in the darkness with his hat pulled low over his face and his collar turned up.

'This is a stick-up, watch out!' Ventre yelled into Moroh's ear.

Lottie had also spotted the suspicious figure and had sprung open the rear door of the car.

'Get in,' she yelled.

Ventre pushed Moroh towards the car, but the latter was wise to the pair's motives. He slammed the door shut with his foot and lunged at Ventre, shoving him into the advancing shadow, whom he recognised as Guarino. He turned on his heels and sprinted towards Westchester Avenue, followed by a hail of bullets. One of these wild shots struck an innocent bystander who had been blathering with her friends. Millie Schwartz's only crime was that she had been in the wrong place at the wrong time.

Charge sheets against Lottie, Guarino and Ventre were expedited on the strength of Moroh's testimony. Moroh himself was taken before County Judge Harry Stackwell to be held as a material witness in the case. He objected to the bail of $25,000 that was set for him and protested at being incarcerated for his own safety.

'But these people might try to have someone intimidate you,' advised Judge Stackwell.

'They have no one to back them up,' Moroh scoffed, indicating perhaps that Lottie's star had waned considerably in the underworld.

Nevertheless, it was deemed safer to hold him in the

material-witness section of the county jail. On 27 June, indictments were returned by the grand jury.

'Convinced that by the capture of the trio we had broken up a nucleus for a gang that was being trained to avenge the death of Vincent Coll, we secured additional indictments for robbery in the event that the murder charge should fall through,' Chief Assistant District Attorney for Bronx County Sylvester Ryan later wrote.

On 15 February, almost two years to the day after the truncation of her husband's trunk call, Lottie Coll went on trial for murder in the first degree. In an article that he penned for the May 1935 edition of *True Detective Mysteries*, Sylvester Ryan, who presented the people's case along with Assistant District Attorney George Tilzer, described Lottie's cold, calculating exterior and her refusal to play ball:

> Lottie Coll had persistently refused to talk about her participation in the crime. Dressed in a new spring outfit, she came into court and coyly played a game of hide and seek with press photographers as the jury was picked.

As the trial proceeded and the testimony of Moroh was put on the record, however, she began to lose some of her assurance. A woman and her husband, both friends of Lottie's, were ordered to stay out of the courtroom when it was reported that they had made signs to Moroh as he testified. During the morning recess of the eleventh day, Lottie held a conference with her attorney, H. Bennett Salomon, and when she returned to the courtroom her face was pasty white beneath her makeup. As she waited until the judge was seated, she rocked unsteadily on her feet. Her head was bent low and tears were welling in her eyes. When she sat down she began to sob uncontrollably.

Shortly after this, the court adjourned for lunch and the cause of Lottie's sudden breakdown was revealed. Guarino was convinced that the mass of testimony was against him and begged his companions to plead guilty to lesser charges so that he might escape the chair. The thought of how the jury would react to the overwhelming evidence that was amassed against him over the previous eleven days had instilled the fear of God into him. Convinced that he was destined to be sentenced to death, he made a statement admitting that he had a personal grudge against 'Dugie' – Moroh – and absolved the others from any intent to kill. From the people's viewpoint, it seemed foolish not to allow a plea of guilty. On 26 February, as a result of his statement, a mistrial was declared and Guarino pleaded guilty to second-degree murder. Both Lottie Coll and Joseph Ventre pleaded guilty to manslaughter. Bennett Salomon told the court that his client was innocent but that she was sacrificing herself to save Guarino's life.

Chief Assistant District Attorney Sylvester Ryan concurred in the motions. He declared that the evidence relating to the hold-up was necessary to convict Lottie and Ventre but that Guarino's confession that he had carried out the shooting as a result of a personal vendetta against Moroh made it doubtful whether the pair would be found guilty. He told the court that he believed Lottie and Ventre were morally guilty and that it would be unfair for Guarino to take all the blame for the crime. He claimed that Guarino's infatuation with Lottie had prompted him to make his confession and accept the blame. It emerged that the police were of the opinion that Lottie schooled and dominated her two co-defendants after associates of her dead husband had refused to consort with her.

'The case presents a difficult question of law and fact,' said Judge Stackwell. 'This is a well-qualified plea, meeting with the best interests of law and justice.'

Entering a lesser plea of manslaughter, as opposed to the original charge of first-degree murder, was a bitter pill for Lottie to swallow. She had maintained a wall of silence from the beginning and had planned to tell the jury that she had been framed by the police because she was the widow of a notorious gangster. Fighting back the tears, she could barely speak through her leathery grimace as she gave her personal details to the court clerk. Even at her weakest, Lottie nurtured delusions of grandeur, telling the court she was a twenty-five-year-old fashion designer.

A fortnight later, she was languishing in Bedford Reformatory on a sentence of six to twelve years. Any suggestion that Lottie acted unselfishly to save her latest suitor from the chair would be fatuous in the extreme. Though he shared her bed, Guarino was never more than her underling. There is little doubt that her hand had been forced on this occasion, and no amount of loyalty to her lover would soften the blow. During her initial detention she showed bitterness against her two co-defendants, whom she accused of 'talking'. One saving grace, however, was that she may have been spared a more severe censure if, as suspected, she had had a hand in crimes of a more serious nature, for even the toughest nuts tended to sing while on death row. Guarino was given twenty years to life in Sing Sing and Ventre was handed a term of seven-and-a-half to fifteen years. Once again, association with Lottie had resulted in tragedy for her acolytes.

*

Lottie did her stint in prison, though it is unclear exactly how long she was inside for. Her fervour was undimmed by time, however. With the Second World War looming, she contributed to the war effort by breaking into and robbing a post office. Using the assumed name of Elizabeth Whitner, she was soon apprehended and was hauled before the courts on 2 July 1943. She pleaded guilty. Ignoring her high rate of recidivism, Judge Murray Hulbert imposed a suspended sentence on her and fixed the period of probation supervision at five years. After that, she spent the following three years living at 966 East 181st Street. A bench warrant for her arrest was issued on 15 August 1946, as she had failed to report to her probation officer for the previous three months. Her whereabouts remained a mystery from then on. Over the next twenty years, probation officer Arch Sayler searched diligently for her but found no clues as to where she might have fled to. As the Criminal Identification Bureau of the NYPD and the FBI had reported no arrests since she had been placed on probation, Sayler surmised that 'It would serve no useful purpose to continue the search for this woman.' On 14 May 1965, the District Court of the Southern District of New York dismissed the petition and vacated the bench warrant that had been issued in 1946. There was neither sight nor sound of Lottie Kreisberger-Coll from that day forth.

EPILOGUE

It was small wonder that Vincent Coll's relatives took offence at the proposed screening of *Mad Dog Coll* in the Astor Cinema in na Doirí Beaga back in 1962. Burt Balaban's black-and-white film distorted the facts of the dead gangster's life beyond all recognition and portrayed Coll as a slavering psychotic who got a hard-on at the idea of killing. As if his criminal reputation was not substantial enough already, the film even contained the hint of a rape scene, a crime of which he had never been accused. Such embellished accounts only serve to perpetuate the dark myth of Mad Dog Coll.

It is well-nigh impossible, however, to weave a coherent picture of Coll from the tangled filaments of the past. He was a spontaneous criminal who lacked either fear or morality and expressed his rage, greed and sense of adventure through his trigger finger. Yet he was a loving husband, a faithful brother and a suave leader of men. People who knew Coll spoke fondly of him. He abounded in charms and gladdened and saddened in equal measure. It was this blend of musicality and menace that made him, according to author Peter Quinn, the prototypical Bowery Boyo – later immortal-ised in the films of James Cagney.

Despite all his seductive aplomb, Coll's career was

categorised by savage acts of random killing. As a reckless marauder, he was more feared for his moxie than for his intellect. The inner ferment of his shattered mind may be attributable to a Dickensian childhood, but when he breached gangster protocol by shooting a woman (May Smith) and a child (Michael Vengelli) even the outlaws chose to outlaw him. Such was his legacy that author T. J. English charts a connection between Vincent and the notorious Westies, who terrorised the West Side of Manhattan during the 1970s and 1980s. English writes that 'Within that world, if he wasn't known by name, he was known by legend and temprament.'

Historically, Vincent Coll marked the end of the line for Irish gangsters. Before Prohibition, the New York underworld was dominated by disorganised rural gangs like the Whyos, the Plug Uglies, the Gophers, the Kerryonians, the Dead Rabbits and the Hudson Dusters. With the birth of the Syndicate, however, the balance of power shifted from the street fighter to the white-collar mobster, as bootlegging moved from a neighbourhood concern to a corporate enterprise. It was during this cusp in American criminality that Coll made his lunge for gangland supremacy. It is fair to say that he was ill-equipped to grapple with the evolving landscape of crime, and he paid dearly for his inadequacies. He lacked the polish of the smoother type of gangster that was beginning to emerge, and all his street swagger and wise-guy vernacular could not mask the fact that Vincent Coll still had dirt on his boots.

By the 1930s the Irish in America were beginning to emerge from the severe deprivation and crippling prejudice which had characterised their experiences of the preceding decades. World War II would mark a milestone in Irish assimilation in their adopted country. It had been a slow, painful process, and the scars it had left ran deep. Vincent Coll's wildcat antics only reinforced the stereotype of the fighting Mick that the Irish in America had tried so hard to cast aside. He was seen therefore as having let his country down and was a source of great shame to his own people. It was no coincidence that Mayor Jimmy Walker, the great white hope of Irish America, was one of the first politicians to express outrage at the Harlem Baby Massacre.

Vincent Coll was a mutation of the American Dream and was destined to die in the very streets that had spawned him. Yet his tragedy is as much a part of the Irish-American story as that of the Kennedys. Although he will undoubtedly go down in the black book of Ireland, his misdeeds are long forgotten in his home parish of Gaoth Dobhair. His neighbours and relatives only express sadness at what might have been had his parents not decided to board the ship to New York.

Select Bibliography

Addy, Ted, *Dutch Schultz*, New York, 1973.

Allen, Frederick Lewis, *Only Yesterday*, New York, 1931.

Asbury, Herbert, *The Gangs of New York*, New York, 1928.

Behr, Edward, *Prohibition: Thirteen Years that Changed America*, New York, 1996.

Brode, Douglas, *Money, Women and Guns*, New York, 1995.

Carcaterra, Lorenzo, *Sleepers*, London, 1996.

Cohen, Rich, *Tough Jews*, London, 1998.

Doctorow, E. L., *Billy Bathgate*, New York, 1989.

Douglas, Ann, *Terrible Honesty*, London, 1997.

English, T. J., *The Westies*, New York, 1991.

Feder, Sid and Joesten, Joachim, *The Luciano Story*, New York, 1994.

Gabbler, Neal, *Winchell*, New York, 1994.

Gambino, Richard, *Blood of my Blood: The Dilemma of the Italian-Americans*, Garden City, New York, 1974.

Harris, John, *The Family: A Social History of the Twentieth Century*, New York, 1991.

Johnson, Paul, *A History of the American People*, London, 1997.

Kefauver, Estes, *Crime in America*, Garden City, New York, 1951.

Kennedy, William, *Legs*, New York, 1983.

Kenny, Kevin, *Making Sense of the Molly Maguires*, Oxford, 1998.

Kobler, John, *Capone*, New York, 1971.

Leibowitz, Robert, *The Defender*, Englewood Cliffs, New Jersey, 1981.

Levine, Gary, *Jack 'Legs' Diamond: Anatomy of a Gangster*, New York, 1995.

Lyle, John H., *The Dry and Lawless Years,* Englewood Cliffs, New Jersey, 1960.

Mac Fhionnlaoich, Seán, *Scéal Ghaoth Dobhair,*. Baile Átha Cliath, 1983.

Miller, Kerby A., *Emigrants and Exiles,* Oxford, 1985.

Nash, Jay Robert, *World Encyclopedia of Organized Crime,* London, 1993.

Nic Giolla Bhríde, Cáit, *Stairsheanchas Ghaoth Dobhair,* Baile Átha Cliath, 1996.

Nown, Graham, *The English Godfather,* London, 1987.

Ó Connacháin, Liam, *Niall Mac Giolla Bhríde,* Baile Átha Cliath, 1939.

O'Connor, Richard, *Hell's Kitchen,* Philadelphia and New York, 1958.

Pisciotta, Alexander W., *Benevolent Repression,* New York and London, 1994.

Rockaway, Robert A., *But – He Was Good to His Mother,* Jerusalem, 1993.

Rosen, Victor, *Dark Plunder,* New York, 1955.

Ruth, David E., *Inventing the Public Enemy,* Chicago, 1996.

Sann, Paul, *Kill the Dutchman,* New York, 1971.

Sinclair, Andrew, *Era of Excess: A Social History of the Prohibition Movement,* New York, 1964.

Turkus, Burton B., and Feder, Sid, *Murder, Inc.,* New York, 1992.

Yaquinto, Marilyn, *Pump 'Em Full of Lead,* New York, 1998.

Articles

Jackson, William H., 'Trailing Mad Dog Coll,' in *True Detective Mysteries,* April 1935.

Mac Suibhne, Breandán, 'Soggarth Aroon and Gombeen-Priest: Canon James MacFadden (1842–1917)' in *Radical Irish Priests, 1660–1970,* edited by Gerard Moran, Dublin, 1998.

Ryan, Sylvester, 'Lottie Coll: New York Gun Girl' in *True Detective Mysteries,* May 1935.

INDEX